THE **INCREASE** LIFE

by Tony Scott

THE INCREASE LIFE

by Tony Scott

Published in Toledo, Ohio, by Tony Scott Ministries, Inc. and Eden
Publications.

Cover design by Tri-Point Teleproductions, Inc.

Dedication

At the tender age of eighteen I met the woman of my dreams. She was working in a concession stand at a church youth camp where her parents were counselors. From that day till this, Shirley has always been in and on my heart. She has the intelligence, energy and will to run a large corporation. She has the warmth, grace, beauty, and charm to make the least person on earth feel like royalty.

Because of the way she increases my life and almost every person who is touched by her, this book was able to be written. Her patience, love, and sometimes firm voice and hand continually help us to experience "The Increase Life." While the book bears my name, it is truly the story of our lives. "Her children (Darin and Melony) rise up and call her blessed."

Proverbs 31:29 best describes this woman I call my wife: *"Many women have done wonderful things but you've outclassed them all!"*

Acknowledgements

There are many special people in our lives whose encouragement and assistance have made this book possible:

To our dear friends, Scott & M.J. Michael, who have provided a tremendous platform for sharing these truths.

To our special friends, Dex & Birdie Yager, for incredible opportunities to reach hundreds of thousands of people.

To Susan Webb for going above and beyond to help me write the manuscript.

To MaryAnn Opal for reading and editing the manuscript.

To Joni Allinson and Tri-Point Teleproductions, Inc. for copy formatting and cover design.

To Beth Strachn for final editing.

To Pat Lehman who graciously accepted the assignment to intercede for me on a daily basis.

To the Cathedral of Praise Family for loving us and allowing us the privilege of shepherding them for 27+ years.

Contents

Introduction: There's More! 7

1. The Promise of Unlimited Supply 17

2. The Promise of Increase 25

3. Experiencing the Promise of Forgiveness 35

4. Our Part in Acting on God's Promises: Obedience 41

5. Our Part in Acting on God's Promises: Fruitfulness 51

6. Our Part in Acting on God's Promises: Giving 57

7. Giving and Increase—The Bigger Picture 67

8. The Promise of Debt-Free Living 79

9. The Promise of God's Timing in Increase 89

10. The Increase We Can Experience As We "Wait" 99

11. The Promise of Many Methods of Multiplication 109

12. The Place of Your Increase 115

13. Challenges on the Way to Increase 133

14. Enlargement after Sacrifice 147

15. Choosing Increase 159

16. Increase Out of Decrease 165

17. Responding to Increase 175

    Conclusion: Still More 185

Foreword

At last a book on the abundant life which gives the balanced message of *The Increase Life*. Birdie and I have been richly blessed by the lives and ministry of Tony and Shirley Scott and their family for many years. We are honored to call them our friends and to be affiliated with their ministry.

This book should be read and studied by everyone who desires to achieve success and live their dreams. Success involves more than just money. Success should abound in our whole life – every part of it – body, soul and spirit. Over the years, though we were often criticized for our commitment to build an increase life, time has proven that it is God's will for us and everyone who will believe and practice His principles.

The Increase Life is filled with life-changing principles which have been experienced first-hand by the Scott family. His daughter, Melony, is married to Diamond IBO Dave Bradley and lives in Auckland, NZ. His son, Darin, is married to Bronwyn and together they travel with Soul'd Out singing at functions around the world. Their lives personify the message and theme of this book.

Scott's message is so needed in the body of Christ at this hour in history. It will help you develop the understanding of that extraordinary "increased life." Get ready to experience an awesome journey into *The Increase Life* as you read the heartwarming stories and principles of this book.

Dexter & Birdie Yager

Introduction

There's More!

Increase.

Prosperity.

Success.

We often use these words interchangeably. Numerous books are available on all three subjects. So why another book on this topic?

Because there's *more* to the message of increase and prosperity than most people have heard!

The *whole* message of the Bible about increase is a message about *whole-life increase*—every area of your life, all of your life. The Bible message about increase has to do with who you are and who you *become*. It has to do with what you do with the natural talents and spiritual gifts that God gives to you. It has to do with the influence you have, the leadership you exert, and the things you accomplish for God's Kingdom. It has to do with resources only to the extent that resources are a necessary part of living and a necessary part of *extending* or increasing the Kingdom of God.

Too often we limit our concepts of "increase" or "success" to our finances, assets portfolio, or possessions. God's increase is for the totality of a person's life. It *includes* finances but it is never limited to finances. Increase includes an increase in wisdom and knowledge, faith, ability and capacity and capability, energy and vitality and health, love and joy and peace. It includes increase in manifestations of all the fruit of the Spirit and an increase in the flow of spiritual gifts. Genuine increase touches all areas of a person's life. One area of life cannot be significantly increased unless all other areas of a person's life are also increased.

Four Distinctive Hallmarks
of the Increase Message

There are four main ways in which the message of whole-life increase differs from the message of many success teachers.

1. Genuine increase is a process.

"Prosperity" is often taught as a result or a resulting consequence, and many times prosperity is presented as an event or a specific act of "receiving."

"Increase" is a life-long process. It occurs because we are faithful to God's commandments, including His commandment to give, week in and week out, month in and month out, year in and year out. We are faithful in good times and bad. The trend is one that, overall, is *upward, onward, forward*, and *enlarged*. We may have down times, dry spells, or discouraging moments, but the overall trend of our lives is a positive one of increase. We are to be ever-growing in an understanding of who we are and why we were placed on this earth, in our knowledge of God, and in our fruitfulness and usefulness to God's Kingdom.

We are designed for growth from the first moments of our creation. We *grow* from a fetus to a baby to a child to an adult. We are not made to be diminished or decreased. Parallel to our natural growth, we are to grow in wisdom, understanding, knowledge, and spiritual authority. Jesus grew both in physical stature and in spiritual strength. (See Luke 1:80.)

Not only did God design us for increase, but apparently all other aspects of His creation as well. Astronomers tell us that when light first "began," those rays of light entered into outer space and kept moving. The only thing that stops their motion is if they hit objects, such as a planet, asteroid, or meteor. The original rays from the light of creation, if they haven't hit something, are still moving. This is the basis for an entire theory of an expanding universe. The universe is growing at a rate of 186,000 miles per second (which is the speed of light), far faster than we can begin to keep up with its growth!

Everything in God's Word is about the processes of life. We find from cover to cover in the Bible the annual feasts and rituals being lived out—year after year. We find

> *We are designed for growth from the first moments of our creation. We grow from a fetus to a baby to a child to an adult. We are not made to be diminished or decreased.*

the Scriptures being read consistently—year after year. We find people giving and bringing their offerings to God—year after year.

At no time do we find an example held up to us of a person who wanders into a religious meeting, gives a hundred-dollar offering, and becomes an overnight millionaire as a result. God does not operate by the lottery system. The glitter and hype of the instant-payoff prosperity message simply doesn't produce lasting results for the vast majority of people who have heard it and "tried" it with an offering or two.

2. Genuine increase results in *eternal* riches as well as temporal material blessings.

The message of prosperity tends to be calculated in terms of numbers, dollars, amounts, and sizes of "toys" and possessions.

The message of increase is incalculable. It is inner, eternal, and beyond measure. How much love is enough? How much joy is sufficient? How much peace is adequate? The true riches of life are intangible.

How much health is "good" health? How much friendship is "quality" friendship? How many souls won to the Kingdom of God are "enough" souls?

9

There is never too much of the things we value the most! The prosperity message tends to end in material gold.

The increase message ends in God's goals, which are always expressed in terms that have an eternal quality to them. Notice the words the Bible uses in describing the palm tree in Psalm 92:12—"long-lived, stately, upright, useful, and fruitful." The psalm continues that the person who is planted in God's house is the person who grows "like a cedar in Lebanon [majestic, stable, durable, and incorruptible]."

That's the life God desires for us to have. It is a life of *whole-person* increase, not a life in which our bank account, portfolio, or real-estate holdings are increased and the rest of our life languishes and withers.

In III John 2, which is often used by prosperity teachers, it proclaims, "Beloved, I pray that you may prosper in every way and [that your body] may keep well, even as [I know] your soul keeps well and prospers." *Prosper in EVERY WAY.* Note how that letter of John continues: "I greatly rejoiced when [some of] the brethren from time to time arrived and spoke [so highly] of the sincerity and fidelity of your life, as indeed you do live in the Truth [the whole Gospel presents]." (III John 3)

> *If you genuinely want all that is associated with increase, prosperity, and success, you must focus on things inside you, not factors that lie outside you.*

John rejoiced in the *fidelity*—the faithfulness and consistency—of the believer. He rejoiced in the fact that they were living out the Gospel in every area of their lives—and he prayed they would have physical, material, and natural health that matched their spiritual health.

Those who believe that Bible prosperity is primarily natural, physical, material, or financial are in error. So, too, are those who believe Bible prosperity is primarily spiritual. The Bible does not separate the material and spiritual. The term prosperity relates to the totality of a person's life. The material and spiritual are united because man is a material creature—or natural, fleshly, physical creature—as well as a spiritual creature.

3. Genuine increase flows from the inside out.

The prosperity message tends to say that a miracle is on its way to you—external to you and coming toward you—and in that miracle lies your increase.

The *increase* message of God's Word is exactly the opposite. The increase begins within you—the miracle is internal and born of the Holy Spirit residing in you—and that increase spills over into your natural and material life. It overflows from your spirit into your attitude, words, and behavior. It overflows into your physical and emotional life in the form of motivation, enthusiasm, energy, stamina, and strength. It overflows from your behavior into your work, your relationships, your ministry, and, in turn, it overflows into material, financial, and natural increase.

Most people are externally motivated. They look outside themselves to see things, from houses to cars to airplanes, as their motivation for working hard at a job. Sometimes the external motivation is recognition or expressions of appreciation from people who matter to them. Sometimes the external motivation is a raise in status or a promotion at work.

I believe the *correct* motivation for genuine life changes is *internal*, not external. It is when we seek to fulfill God's plan for our lives—and we are willing to make changes in our lives so we line up our attitudes, beliefs, and behaviors with God's plan— that we find genuine satisfaction, purpose, and joy. Internal motivation is at the heart of true change.

Internal factors are vital for lasting "behavioral modification." If you genuinely want *all* that is associated with increase, prosperity, and success, you must focus on things inside you, not factors that lie outside you.

4. Genuine increase is rooted in community.

The prosperity message too often begins and ends with self. The increase message is one that always includes others and is aimed at the benefit of those in need.

The Bible teaches that the place to experience maximum increase is a place of fellowship and mutual worship with other believers. The psalmist gives us a clear message that we are to be rooted in a particular *place* that God designates for us. It is there that we are to praise God, give thanks to God, and serve God. It is there that we "flourish like the palm tree [be long-lived, stately, upright, useful, and fruitful]." (Ps. 92:12)

The New Testament builds on this principle. The apostle Paul wrote to the Thessalonians:

> May the Lord make you to increase and excel and overflow in love for one another and for all people, just as we also do for you,
>
> So that He may strengthen and confirm and establish your hearts faultlessly pure and unblamable in holiness in the sight of our God and Father, at the coming of our Lord Jesus Christ (the Messiah) with all His saints (the holy and glorified people of God)! Amen, (so be it)!" (I Thess. 3:12–13)

Throughout the Scriptures, the Lord refers to a special increase that will occur prior to the return of our Lord Jesus Christ. That increase will include material wealth primarily for the purpose of bringing about the greatest revival the world has ever known. As part of that increase, the Kingdom of God will experience a great outpouring of God's healing power, a great outpouring of praise and joy, and a great outpouring of love among Christian believers of different denominations and races and cultures.

More praise.

More prayer.

More miracles.

More resources.

More outreaches.

More souls saved.

More needs met.

More lives blessed.

The increase of God's Kingdom is an all-encompassing increase. In Ephesians 2:21 we read, "In Him the whole structure is joined (bound, welded) together harmoniously, and it continues to rise (grow, increase) into a holy temple in the Lord [a sanctuary dedicated, consecrated and sacred to the presence of the Lord]." God increases the *whole* of His people. He does this for *His* purposes and *His* glory.

Ultimately, that increase within the Body of Christ overflows in the form of outreach to those who are lost and in need of God's deliverance and salvation. As Isaiah 29:18–19 tells us: "In that day shall the deaf hear the words of the book, and out of obscurity and gloom and darkness the eyes of the blind shall see. The meek also shall increase their joy in the Lord, and the poor among men shall rejoice and exult in the Holy One of Israel."

Increase Begins and Ends in God

The richness of His grace.

The richness of His goodness.

The richness of His love.

We find repeatedly in the Scriptures the vast wealth of God's presence with us. We are wise to desire His presence more than we desire life itself. Our joy and our full sense of purpose and satisfaction in life reside in our relationship with the Lord. In Him is our *abundant life.*

The increase message, from start to finish, is rooted in a person's *relationship* with God Almighty.

In giving the Law, God spoke repeatedly of the abiding relationship He desired to have with His people. In Leviticus 26:9 Moses tells the Israelites God is "leaning toward you with favor and regard for you." His presence will be one of continual blessing on their behalf. Every aspect of their life will be blessed because He will give His people the total blessing available in

---

In Leviticus 26:9 Moses tells the Israelites God is "leaning toward you with favor and regard for you."

His presence. All of His wisdom will be available to them to enlighten them, all of His power will be available to them to protect them, and all of His provision will be available to them to enrich them. All that God is He will bestow upon them to the extent they can receive it.

What God gives to His people will, in turn, infuse them with His energy and His life to the extent they will be fruitful and multiply.

Jesus echoed this promise of His *presence* in saying to His disciples, "I came that they may have and enjoy life, and have it in abundance (to the full, till it overflows)." (John 10:10)

The apostle John summarized the benefit of Christ's presence by saying, "In Him was Life, and the Life was the Light of men." (John 1:4)

Throughout the Scriptures, God gives us His presence because He desires to *bless* His people and to increase them. God wants His people to be a delightful, winsome people. He wants us to be blessed so we can be a blessing. In that, God receives glory and honor. Our blessings bring benefit to God. They reveal to others that God is the Source of all that is good and beneficial, the Source of all that is valuable and worthy, and the Source of all that deserves honor and praise.

What always begins with dependence upon God ends with praise to God for His dependability in caring for His people!

Do You Truly Desire Increase?

Are you looking for a quick-fix formula to material success? This book is not for you.

Do you desire genuine *increase* in the totality of your life? Do you desire to grow in your relationship with God your Creator and the Provider of all you need? Read on!

Chapter 1

The Promise of Unlimited Supply

My mother was my hero. What I know about God I learned primarily from my mother—both in word and by example. She had a covenant with God that was deeply rooted in a personal faith. She understood that she belonged to God, and that He had pledged Himself to her. She *knew* deep within her heart that God would never leave her nor forsake her, that she was never alone, and that God's pledge to her was abiding and unending.

My mother was a mill worker and many times faced cut-backs and lay-offs on her job. We would ask her, "How are we going to make it?" Mom would reply, "God is our Source. The mill is not our source. God will take care of us."

My mother had never heard a minister use those words. They came from her own understanding of God. She taught me that God not only had an unlimited supply of blessings, but He had *all* methods at His fingertips and that He could deliver His supply to us in a thousand or more ways.

Never make corporate America your source.
Never make the government your source.
Never make the stock market your source.
Never make a potential family inheritance your source.
God alone desires to be your Source.

A Supply of All Good Things

All blessings come from God. He is incapable of giving "bad" gifts—all of His gifts are for our eternal good. Furthermore, *all* things that we know as good come from His hand regardless of whether we acknowledge Him as the Source. James 1:17 tells us plainly, "Every good gift and every perfect (free, large, full) gift is from above; it comes down from the Father of all [that gives] light, in [the shining of] Whom there can be no variation [rising or setting] or shadow cast by His turning [as in an eclipse]."

It is the Lord who pours out blessings—material and physical, mental and emotional—*and* spiritual "good things."

The prophet Joel prophesied the material and spiritual nature of God's blessings in saying:

> Be glad then, you children of Zion, and rejoice in the Lord, your God; for He gives you the former or early rain in just measure and in righteousness, and He causes to come down for you the rain, the former rain and the latter rain, as before.
>
> And the [threshing] floors shall be full of grain and the vats shall overflow with juice [of the grape] and oil.
>
> And I will restore or replace for you the years that the locust has eaten—the hopping locust, the stripping locust, and the crawling locust, My great army which I sent among you.
>
> And you shall eat in plenty and be satisfied and praise the name of the Lord, your God. (Joel 2:23–26)

Oh, that we might partake of ALL God's blessings! From start to finish, His supply is one of goodness.

A Supply Without Limits

If you search the Scriptures, you will find that God used the word "Almighty" fifty-seven times in referring to Himself.

Almighty is a word that refers to His self-sufficiency. He needs nothing and no one because He is all and all. He has *all* might, *all* power, *all* wisdom, *and all* ability. He is God without any limitations and without need.

We are the ones who limit what we receive from God. He is a God *without* limitations on either Himself or on the blessings He desires to bestow on His people.

In leading the Israelites from Egyptian bondage to the land of promise, God performed miracle after miracle on their behalf. It was a series of miracles that caused Pharaoh to allow them to leave the land. It was a miracle that the Israelites were given wealth from their former oppressors to ensure they would leave in peace and not return. It was a miracle that brought them across the Red Sea. It was a miracle that water came from a rock and manna fell from the sky.

In Psalm 78 we find a summary of the mighty deeds that God did on behalf of the Israelites, and yet again and again we find the refrain of rebellion: "They kept not the covenant"..."They still went on to sin against Him"..."they tempted God in their hearts"..."They remembered not"..."They lied to Him with their tongues. For their hearts were not right or sincere with Him, neither were they faithful and steadfast to His covenant."

The Israelites experienced some of the most powerful miracles in the history of all mankind and, even so, they *limited* God. They did not comprehend His absolute righteousness or power. They did not comprehend His infinite love for them and His provision for them.

They had a small idea of God and they reacted to life with a narrowness of outlook and a meager understanding of God's nature.

We, too, tend to limit God. We set limits on the areas of our lives in which we will allow Him to rule and reign. We set boundaries on His prosperity. Some err in placing the boundaries of His prosperity solely around the spiritual nature of man; others err by putting boundaries on prosperity that limit His blessings to the material or financial realm of life.

God desires that we set no limits! He is not bound to our time frame. Nor is He bound to our methods. God is not bound to just one area of our life. He deals with us in the wholeness of our humanity, the entire length of our days, and in the methods and means that are of His choosing, in His timing, and for His eternal purposes.

You cannot have a genuine encounter with the Almighty God, King of this entire universe, and come away from that encounter the same person.

In writing to the Romans, the apostle Paul said, "Oh, the depth of the riches and wisdom and knowledge of God! How unfathomable (inscrutable, unsearchable) are His judgments (His decisions)! And how untraceable (mysterious, undiscoverable) are His ways (His methods, His paths)! For who has known the mind of the Lord and who has understood His thoughts, or who has [ever] been His counselor?" (Rom. 11:33–34)

In writing to the Ephesians, Paul wrote that he had been authorized by God "to proclaim to the Gentiles the unending (boundless, fathomless, incalculable, and exhaustless) riches of Christ [wealth which no human being could have searched out]." (Eph. 3:8)

You cannot have a genuine encounter with the Almighty God, King of this entire universe, and come away from that encounter the same person. God *changes* you any time you come into His presence. He transforms you, enriches you, and blesses you. Or if you are in rebellion and you come close to Him, He chastises you and convicts you. Either way, you are changed in some way. The truth of His judgments, commandments, and statutes enlightens you and gives you guidance. His love comforts you. His mercy compels your praise and thanksgiving.

Why are so many blinded to the unlimited nature of God and the unlimited resources He desires to make available to His people? Because the "god of this world has blinded the unbelievers' minds [that they should not discern the truth], preventing them from seeing the illuminating light of the Gospel of the glory of Christ (the Messiah), Who is the Image and Likeness of God." (II Cor. 4:4)

The god of this world—Satan—will do everything in his power to keep you from comprehending and appreciating what God wants to do in your life. The last thing he wants is for you to catch a glimpse of all that you can be in Christ Jesus and all that the Father has for you.

The apostle Paul encouraged the Romans, "Do not be conformed to this world (this age), [fashioned after and adapted to its external, superficial customs], but be transformed (changed) by the [entire] renewal of your mind [by its new ideals and its new attitude], so that you may prove [for yourselves] what is the good and acceptable and perfect will of God, even the thing which is good and acceptable and perfect [in His sight for you]." (Rom. 12:2)

Be not conformed! Don't allow yourself to be blinded into limiting God!

How Far Can You See?

I recently was driving through Tennessee and noticed a large billboard just outside Chattanooga that said, "See Seven States from Rock City." There is a mountain in Rock City that provides a panoramic view, and from that vantage point one can see seven different states.

God said to Abraham, "I will give you all that you see." Abraham still had to walk out the land, but the promise of God was that he would receive all that he saw.

In Ephesians 3:20, God gives us a similar Word. He says that He will give us "far over and above all that we [dare] ask or think [infinitely beyond our highest prayers, desires, thoughts, hopes, or dreams]." What is it that you can see in your mind's eye? What is it that you see with your spiritual eyes? What is it that you see in your dreams, your hopes, your prayers? What *vision* has God given you for your future?

Your mind-set—the view you have of God and of your own life embedded in God—determines your "life set." If you're a small thinker, you achieve little stuff. If you're a big thinker, you get big things done. The bigger your concept of the God who dwells within you, the greater your concept of what is *possible* for you to accomplish. Paul wrote to the Philippians, "I have strength for all things in Christ Who empowers me." (Phil. 4:13)

All things. Paul put no limits on God's ability to work things out in him, through him, and all about him. He had faith in a very big God—a God unlimited in power and majesty.

You may not have all the ability you think you need. But God has the ability.

You may not have all of the education you think you need. But God has the knowledge, wisdom, and understanding.

You may not have the social status or power you think you need. But God has all the power and all the means at His disposal.

Has God ever lost a battle?

Has God ever been defeated?

Has God ever been taken by surprise?

No!

And who is it that lives in you? If you have accepted Christ Jesus as your Savior, you are indwelled by the Holy Spirit of Almighty God. He desires to manifest Himself in you, through you, and on your behalf *if you will only open your mind and heart to the unlimited nature of His power, provision, and presence.*

When you limit God, you limit yourself.

Ask God today to give you a revelation of Himself. In doing so, He will give you a revelation of *yourself* and all that He has for you.

The more you discover about God, the more you discover your own potential. God made you in *His* image—with a God-consciousness and a self-awareness and a world-awareness. He made you a thinking, feeling, believing spirit being in a physical body to live in a natural world that He created. God designed

---

When you limit God,
you limit yourself.

---

you to walk and talk with Him and to exert authority over the world He made.

Adam and Eve felt no hesitancy, distance, or shame in the presence of God until they rebelled against God's commandments. Those who believe in Christ Jesus should not feel any hesitancy, distance, or shame in God's presence if they have received His forgiveness for their sin and have been restored to Him through their belief in Jesus Christ as their Savior. God desires for us to be in *relationship* with Him, and He desires for us to do what He authorized Adam and Eve to do—to have dominion over this earth, to subdue it, to enjoy it, and to multiply in it.

God has for every person a revelation about Himself and also a revelation about *ourself.* God desires to reveal to us who we are in His eyes—how He loves us and longs to be in a deep personal relationship with us. He also desires to reveal to us what it is that He has designed for us to do with our lives.

Jeremiah 29:11 tells us: "For I know the thoughts and plans that I have for you, says the Lord, thoughts and plans for welfare and peace and not for evil, to give you hope in your final outcome."

God's plan for us is always a plan for our ultimate and eternal *good.* His plan for us is success, not failure. His plan is for health, not sickness. His plan is for eternal life, not everlasting death. His plan is for increase, not decrease.

His Hand or Yours?

The story is told of a ten-year-old boy who was helping his father with the harvest of their cherry orchard. His father said to him, "Son, make sure you get every cherry from the tree. Times are tough and we need every bit of this fruit."

The boy was diligent in his work, picking every piece of fruit from the tree and carefully transferring it to his bucket, then dumping his full buckets into a larger bin at the end of the row of cherry trees. As the day turned to dusk his father said to him, "Son, did you eat any of the cherries?" The boy replied honestly, "No. Every cherry went into my bucket and then into the bin."

His father said, "Good job! As a reward, I want you to reach into the bin now. Whatever you can scoop up in your hand, that can be yours to eat."

The boy looked at his hand and then looked at his father's hand and said, "Dad, I'd rather you reach in and get me a handful of fruit."

Your heavenly Father invites you to partake of the goodness of the harvest. Are you willing to trust Him to give you what He desires for you to have? It will be so much more than you can secure on your own!

Chapter 2

The Promise of Increase

God does not deal in formulas, but there does seem to be a progression that occurs in the lives of those who experience increase. That progression always begins with a *promise* of increase.

A person may receive a word directly from the Lord about what He desires to do in their life. This word may be received as a person reads the Scriptures—a verse or passage may seem to impact a person's heart in a special way. It may be a word pronounced over the person by someone functioning in the gift of prophecy. It may be a word spoken as part of a message to God's people as a whole that the individual recognizes is applicable to his personal life. Whatever the *method* of delivery, the word is one that the person knows is from God.

For that promise to be genuine, it must be in alignment with the written Word of God. God will not give a person a direct word that in any way contradicts His existing Word, the Bible. All "personal" words must be completely in line with the truth of the Bible.

Our Response to God's Promises

Our response to God's promises is a simple one: We must *believe* God's promises are true—and not only true in a general sense, but true for us personally. We must believe that God's promises are directly applicable to our own lives.

Believing, of course, is another word for *faith*. Faith puts us into position to receive God's provision, protection, and purpose.

Our faith is required in several areas but, first and foremost, we must believe for *what* it is that God has said He is going to provide or accomplish.

In many cases, we believe for too little. We put a cap on what we believe God might do in our lives or in the lives of our loved ones. We know God is great and awesome and knows all things and has all power, but we aren't sure He knows our name and will use His power on our behalf.

We know God is capable of doing all things; we just aren't quite sure what He desires to do for us.

We know God can heal, but we question whether He will heal us and make us whole.

We know God performs great miracles of provision, but we doubt whether He will grant one of those miracles to us.

We know God has all the answers, but we wonder how He will show us His answer to our question, His solution to our need.

Faith is necessary if we are to believe not only that God is capable, but that God *desires* to fulfill His Word in our individual lives. Faith is necessary if we are to personalize the universal promises of God.

We can limit the degree to which God fulfills His promises in us, and the amount of the increase we experience, by a lack of faith. We can short-change ourselves by not believing for ALL that God desires to give us or do on our behalf.

Conversely, the greater our faith and the more steadfast our trust in what God has promised to us, the greater the fulfillment of God's promises and the greater the increase in our lives.

We must continually call ourselves to a position before the Lord by saying, "I trust You, heavenly Father, to give me Your

---

God will only increase you to the level
of your spiritual integrity.

26

best in Your timing and according to Your methods... and always for Your glory and the furtherance of Your Kingdom. I trust You to use Your means and to act in the fullness of time as You see it. I trust You to give me *all* that I need to be and do *all* that You desire."

It is through faith that we put ourselves into the exact position for receiving exactly what God wants to give us, exactly when He wants us to have it.

Spiritual Integrity Establishes the Ceiling

God will only increase you to the level of your spiritual integrity. Your level of maturity in the Lord is directly related to the amount of authority and responsibility and provision God pours out to you.

The worst thing that can happen to any person is to be elevated into a position he cannot handle—to be given responsibilities and authority that he does not know how to shoulder. This can cause great damage to the person, to the institution, and ultimately to the Kingdom of God.

Stop to think a moment about how a good parent treats a child. How much money do you entrust to a five-year-old? Probably very little since a five-year-old has not yet acquired good financial judgment—he doesn't know how to spend money wisely or invest money prudently. When your child is ten years old, you probably entrust him with a little larger "allowance." Over the years, as your child grows and develops and shows you he can handle money wisely, you are likely to give him more and more financial "power." You might even allow your teenager to take your credit card to the mall or give your teen the checks to an account that you fund when he goes off to college. The more evidence you see that your child is handling money wisely, the greater your trust level in giving him more money to handle!

This analogy can extend to the spiritual realm. It is to the spiritually mature person that God gives administrative authority over His church. It is to the person who regularly prays and studies the Word that God gives the greater insights into His plans and purposes on the earth.

God does not set people up for failure. We at times set up others for failure. This is often the case when we thrust brand-new believers into the limelight because they are famous or rich or influential in a particular area of our society. God does not do this, however.

Certainly those who are newly born-again often have the greatest zeal and desire to do God's will. They lack maturity, however, in knowing how to direct that zeal and act on their desires. One of our greatest challenges as a believer is to grow up in Christ and become wise in all ways...*and maintain our zeal at the same time!*

The process of spiritual growth is just that—a process. Spiritual maturity doesn't happen overnight. God gives us spiritual gifts and spiritual opportunities to the degree that we have the wisdom and faith and endurance to handle those gifts and to make the most of those opportunities.

God does not put the brakes on any person who desires to grow. Too often He faces the opposite problem—He desires for us to grow up faster than we are willing to grow!

A blessing is not a blessing if it brings you sorrow, destroys your feelings of worthiness before the Lord, or brings you shame. The mishandling of any of God's blessings can turn that blessing into a curse. That is not God's desire for any person. He gives to those who are best able to handle His increase; He gives to those who are the most steadfast in trusting Him. God's blessings flow to those who are growing in their love for the Lord and who are manifesting that love to others.

"But," you may be saying, "there are many people who seem to be receiving all kinds of blessings who aren't at all spiritually mature; in fact, some of them are downright evil."

My response to you would be, "You are probably looking only at the outward show of what that person possesses. The house that person lives in may not be paid for and, in fact, it may have two huge mortgages...and it certainly may not be a happy *home*. The car that person drives may be leased and on the verge of repossession. What do you really know about how that person feels when the lights are out and he is all alone with his doubts, fears, and guilt? What do you really know about the state of that seemingly picture-perfect marriage when the doors are closed and the couple is alone? What do you really know about the relationship that person has with his children, with his parents, with his friends, with his colleagues at work?"

None of us can ever fully see or know a person's motives or the state of their heart. Only God sees us fully as we are.

Furthermore, many people are capable of acquiring possessions using the systems of this world. What you can know with certainty about such possessions is that they are *temporary* possessions at best. There is nothing eternal or truly *valuable* in the eyes of the Lord that is acquired in contradiction to God's commandments and precepts. Only what God authorizes has *lasting* value. The words to the old Gospel song ring true in every case: "Life will soon be past...Only what's done for Christ will last."

The promises of God promote us. They take us from where we are to where He desires us to be.

Building Up Your Faith

Ask God today to help you grow in your faith. Ask Him to reveal to you more of what it is He desires to be to you and to do on your behalf. I believe God is always faithful to answer a humble request for Him to reveal His mercy and loving-kindness.

Moses made such a request of God. He was a man who struggled with the enormity of the task to which the Lord had called him. He was a man who *desired*—yes, even *required*— the presence of God.

Moses reached a place in his walk with the Lord in which he needed more faith. He needed a greater revelation of God and a greater revelation of what God would be to him and what He would do on his behalf.

One day Moses said to the Lord, "If I have found favor in Your sight, show me now Your way, that I may know You...and that I may find favor in Your sight." (Exod. 33:13)

The Lord responded, "My presence shall go with you, and I will give you rest." He also affirmed to Moses, "You have found favor, loving-kindness, and mercy in My sight and I know you personally and by name." (See Exod. 33:14, 17.)

Then we read this passage in Exodus 33:18—"Moses said, I beseech You, show me Your glory."

Moses wanted to *see* God. Up to this time, Moses had *heard* God but he had never seen Him. Moses frequently took his own tent far away from the camp of the Israelites and pitched it and called it the "tent of meeting." When he went into the tent, a pillar of cloud descended and stood at the door of the tent, and the Lord talked with Moses. (See Exod. 33:7–9.) The Bible tells us the "Lord spoke to Moses face to face, as a man speaks to his friend." (Exod. 33:11)

Then came the day when Moses walked down the mount of Sinai with the tablets of God's law only to find the Israelites worshiping a golden calf. In despair and anger, he threw the tablets of stone to the ground and broke them. The Israelites experienced a great plague for their behavior and God said to them, "You are a stiff-necked people! If I should come among you for one moment, I would consume and destroy you. Now therefore [penitently] leave off your ornaments, that I may know what to do with you." The Israelites left off their ornaments, from Mount Horeb onward. (See Exod. 33:5–6.)

Moses went to meet the Lord with a heavy heart. He was at a crisis point in his leadership of the people. He knew the people had sinned a great sin, and he felt responsible for them and ashamed of them at the same time.

> And Moses said, I beseech You, show me Your glory.
> And God said, I will make all My goodness pass before you, and I will proclaim My name,

THE LORD, before you; for I will be gracious to whom I will be gracious, and will show mercy and loving-kindness on whom I will show mercy and loving-kindness.

But, He said, You can not see My face, for no man shall see Me and live.

And the Lord said, Behold, there is a place beside Me, and you shall stand upon the rock,

And while My glory passes by, I will put you in a cleft of the rock and cover you with My hand until I have passed by.

Then I will take away My hand and you shall see My back; but My face shall not be seen. (Exod. 33:18–23)

Notice that little phrase tucked into God's response, "There is a place beside Me, and you shall stand upon the rock."

God assured Moses that He had a *place* for Moses to stand. It was right next to Him and it was rock-solid. It was a place of protection and certainty.

God has just such a place for you and me today.

Just as Moses, we often find ourselves in situations that overwhelm us. We find ourselves frustrated and angry and distraught, and we are forced back into a position before God where we cry out to Him, "I cannot do this without You." It is precisely that position of utter dependence upon God that is *pleasing* to the Lord. He acknowledges the casting of all our cares upon Him by saying, "I am able. I am the Lord. I will be with you and I will give you rest."

Furthermore, God then invites us to occupy a place beside Him—close to Him—and there He will reveal to us the degree of His glory that we are able to accept and receive.

Oh, what a place this is!

To experience the glory of God even to a degree is to know that God is fully capable of handling any situation we bring to Him. It is to know that He holds all things in His hand—that He has all power and all wisdom. It is to know that He is the Lord of every moment and the Lord of all ages. It is to know that He loves with an infinite love and that He is merciful, kind, and generous toward His people.

God did not allow Moses to see His face, but He did allow him to see His backside. The Lord covered Moses with His hand as He passed by so Moses could not see Him. But then, He allowed Moses to see Him "in retrospect."

How often is that the case with us! We do not fully see the presence or glory of God *in* a circumstance or situation. In fact, at times we seem blinded to the presence of God in our darkest and most dire circumstances. We question, "Where is God? Why has He abandoned me?"

The truth is that God is right there with us, as close to us as He has ever been. We simply do not see Him in the moment of our trial.

But then, if we continue to seek the Lord, we discover "in hindsight" that God was with us all along, orchestrating our lives in every detail so that we might have all of the provision and protection we needed, all of the power and wisdom and authority we needed, and all of the resources we needed to accomplish the task to which He had called us. We look back and say, "Oh my! Truly the Lord has been in our midst and in my life. To God be the Kingdom, and the power, and the glory forever!"

In most cases, God does not give us the pre-vision we desire. In most cases, God does not reveal to us what will happen in the future of our lives. Pre-vision can discourage a person from even beginning a task. Pre-vision can be devastating and destructive.

In all cases, God gives us the *provision* we need to accomplish the tasks to which He has called us. He gives us the *provision* of His abiding presence. He gives us a glimpse of Himself in the "past" of our lives so we will trust Him to protect and provide and to be present with us at all times.

If you look back at your life today with an honest searching for how and when and where God has moved in your life, you are going to come to that place where you see God as you have never seen Him before. You are going to have a new revelation about who God is, who you are, and what kind of relationship God desires to have with you. You are going to "see" God with new eyes and a new perspective.

Moses had a complete change of viewpoint after this encounter with God.

The first time Moses went up Sinai to meet with the Lord, he returned with the tablets of the law and then broke them in frustration and dismay. The second time Moses goes up to Sinai to meet with the Lord, he returns with the tablets of the law and he enacts them. Furthermore, his countenance is different the second time he comes down from the mountain. The Bible tells us, "The skin of his face shone and sent forth beams by reason of his speaking with the Lord." (Exod. 34:29)

What made the difference in Moses' leadership style from that meeting with God onward in their wilderness journey? The people hadn't changed. Aaron and Miriam hadn't change. Moses had changed! Moses had experienced an encounter with the living God that replaced his frustration, rejection, and despair. His glimpse of God infused him with new energy, a new hope for the people of Israel, and a resolute steadfastness to establish all of the commandments and dictates of the Lord.

After this experience, Moses never asked the Lord to reveal Himself again. He faced problems in the years that followed, but he did not ask the Lord again to show him His face. This one glorious revelation of the Lord was enough to last him his entire life. He *knew* without doubt that the Lord was with him, that he had a place next to the Lord, and that his identity and relationship with the Lord was established on a firm foundation.

There are few things more important in the life of a believer than coming to this place where you *know* with unshakable certainty that the Lord is with you at all times and in all places, that you have a place next to the Lord, and that your faith is built on an eternal, unmovable foundation. Once you get to that place, you cannot be moved. You know who you are and *Whose* you are. You know the Lord in a way that is personal and intimate—

you may not be able to express exactly how you know what you know about the Lord, but you know that you know!

I have a file folder on my desk that is filled with prophetic words that have been uttered by men and women of God over my life, the life of my family, and the life of my church and ministry. Any time I get discouraged or come to a tough decision or dilemma, I go to that folder and begin to read aloud these prophetic words from the Lord to me. I hold them in the air and wave them before the Lord and say to Him, "Thank You, Lord, that You have given me a glimpse of Who You are and who I am in You. Thank You, Lord, that You have revealed Yourself to me. Thank You, Lord, that Your Word is sealed in my spirit. I will not disbelieve what You have said to me!"

When you know your place in the Lord, your countenance changes, your thought patterns change, your speech changes, and your actions change.

The moment you come to this place of firm resolve that God is with you and you are with God, two things happen to you. First, boldness rises up in your spirit. You feel the energy of that revelation in the depths of your being. You are empowered by the Lord's presence.

Second, demonic spirits begin to flee from you. They will not remain where the Spirit of the Lord is flowing.

When you *know* your place in the Lord, your countenance changes, your thought patterns change, your speech changes, and your actions change.

A revelation from the Lord about His goodness and about His promises to you makes a lasting change in your "faith level" to believe for God's promises.

If you have any doubt today about whether the promises of God are for you, cry out to the Lord. Ask Him to reveal to you His abiding presence and goodness!

Chapter 3

Experiencing the Promise
of Forgiveness

It's one thing to receive a promise from God.

It's another thing to step into that promise.

There is a great difference between believing in a promise of God and stepping into that promise with your faith and then stepping out in action. Those who step *into* a promise are those who actually do what is necessary to receive the fulfillment of the promise. They *act* in response to the promise, and they act as if the promise is for them personally and as though they *will* receive it in God's timing.

The most important promise of God you can step into is God's promise regarding your own forgiveness and salvation. What does forgiveness have to do with increase? Everything!

Whole-life increase belongs only to those who believe in Christ Jesus and who are cleansed by the blood, washed in the waters of baptism, and renewed daily by the Word. The law of increase states that those who believe are the ones who will receive an increase of their entire *life* that extends into eternity.

They are the ones who will receive blessing and a harvest that lies on the inside—a calm to the soul. They are the ones who experience the fullness of the Holy Spirit in their lives. (See Gal. 5:22–23.) The great harvest to the believer includes relationships that are deep and everlasting; a growing wholeness and harmony of spirit, mind, and body; and feelings of satisfaction, fulfillment, and purpose in life.

The world may plant and reap. But the world apart from Christ Jesus does not experience the true inner richness that only Christ can give.

An Invitation to His House

The story of Mephibosheth is one of the most powerful stories of restoration in the Bible.

Mephibosheth was Jonathan's son, the grandson of King Saul. He was five years old when the news came from Jezreel that Saul and Jonathan had been killed. The custom of most kings at that time was that a new king rising to power would kill all of the heirs of the previous king so no claim to the throne could be made by them.

Mephibosheth's nurse feared for his life and picked him up to flee from the palace of Saul. In her haste, she fell and he became lame, a cripple in both feet. He lived in the house of Machir in Lo-debar.

Lo-debar was a desolate place. The name literally means "no pasture." There was no grass, no sowing or reaping, no grazing— it was a desert place and a deserted place. Lo-debar was dry, hot, and barren. It no doubt looked dead to all who passed by. For Mephibosheth it was a place of existence, but no real life.

Consider a moment the state of Mephibosheth. Jonathan was Saul's son and had Saul served the Lord and not disobeyed Him, Jonathan would have been in position to become the next king. Mephibosheth, as Jonathan's son, was the next in line to become king. He was royalty—his destiny appeared to be that of the king's palace. As a young prince, he no doubt ran through the palace of his grandfather, tall and straight and proud to be of royal blood.

Now he finds himself in Lo-debar, lame in both feet, hiding out, fearful that his identity might bring him death. Mephibosheth probably felt as far from being royal and as far from the palace of the king as any person in all of Israel.

Circumstances had dictated to Mephibosheth his position, his identity, his fate.

What Mephibosheth did not know, however, was that Jonathan and David had a covenant. Although he was the king's son, Jonathan knew in his heart that David was chosen by God to be the next king of Israel. Part of the covenant between Jonathan and David involved David giving assurance to Jonathan that he would not kill Jonathan's heirs when David came to power.

Years later, after David was named king over all Israel, he began to ask himself one day, *Is there still anyone left of the house of Saul to whom I may show kindness for Jonathan's sake?* One of Saul's servants, Ziba, was brought to him and David asked him directly, "Is there not still someone of the house of Saul to whom I may show the [unfailing, unsought, unlimited] mercy and kindness of God?" Ziba replied, "Jonathan has yet a son who is lame in his feet." He told David where he could find this young man and David sent men to Lo-debar to bring Mephibosheth to him.

Mephibosheth came to David in fear. He fell on his face before the king and paid him homage, saying, "Behold your servant!"

David replied, "Fear not, for I will surely show you kindness for Jonathan your father's sake, and will restore to you all the land of Saul your father [grandfather], and you shall eat at my table always."

Mephibosheth bowed himself even lower and said, "What is your servant, that you should look upon such a dead dog as I am?" (See II Sam. 9.)

Could any person have any lower self-esteem than Mephibosheth at that moment? Could any person have less hope for his future? Trembling in fear, he regards himself as a dead dog.

Do you find yourself in a similar position today before the Lord? Do you believe that you have sinned to the point where there is no hope for you? Are you fearful of God's judgment— so fearful that you refuse to accept His loving offer of salvation and restoration? Do you believe that all your life is in the past and that the future holds nothing good for you? Have you lost your purpose in living? Have you lost your identity? Do you feel totally estranged from the King of Kings?

Let me assure you, God continues to extend unfailing and unlimited mercy and kindness to you. God loves you with an infinite love and He desires for you to come close to Him and have a place next to Him.

In one day, and in one encounter of reconciliation and mercy, Mephibosheth moved from Lo-debar to the palace of the king. He ate at David's table as one of the king's sons! So did Mephibosheth's own son, Micha.

Not only that, but Ziba was ordered to care for Mephibosheth. He and his sons and servants were ordered to till the land of Saul that David gave to Mephibosheth and to bring in the produce so Mephibosheth could benefit from it. The Bible even points out that Ziba had fifteen sons and twenty servants—all of whom were at the disposal of Mephibosheth.

Mephibosheth had his identity restored, his land restored, and his future secured.

Did Mephibosheth do anything to deserve this place at the king's table? No. All of this came to Mephibosheth because of the mercy of King David and because David was true to the covenant he had made with Jonathan.

Can you do anything to deserve the Lord's forgiveness and mercy and kindness in your life? No! His forgiveness and mercy are offered to you because of the covenant established by Jesus Christ on your behalf. His kindness is extended to you solely because He chooses to bless you with His presence.

Can you do anything to earn through your own works and striving a place next to God? No. He is the One Who sets you in that place at His table.

Stop looking today at the ways in which you are "lame"— your weaknesses, your faults, your past sins. Stop looking today at the desolate, forsaken place in which you find yourself. Stop looking at the circumstances of your life, and start looking to the

King! He longs to seat you next to Himself and to restore you to all that He has designed for you from the foundation of the world!

A Cleansing of Your Soul

God is in the character-changing business. He is in the transformation business. His desire is to change you from who you are, where you are, and what you are right now into the person He created you to be. He desires to change your lackluster life into a life of purpose, meaning, and great fulfillment. He desires to change you from "just getting by" to living in whole-person increase that begins in your spirit and manifests itself in your mind, body, and material life.

God's desire for you is whole-person, whole-life increase. The key to that increase lies in your receiving God's free offer of forgiveness and salvation.

I invite you today to receive the Lord Jesus Christ into your life. Confess to God that you are a sinner. Ask Him to forgive you and to restore you to right relationship with Him. Ask Him to help you live a new life empowered by His presence within you.

I assure you...He *will* hear and answer you!

Chapter 4

Our Part in Acting on
God's Promises: Obedience

A king named Balak once asked a prophet named Balaam to curse the Israelites. He promised him great riches and honor if he would do so. Balaam, however, responded,

> How can I curse those God has not cursed? Or how can I [violently] denounce those the Lord has not denounced....
> God is not a man, that He should tell or act a lie, neither the son of man, that He should feel repentance or compunction [for what He has promised]. Has He said and shall He not do it? Or has He spoken and shall He not make it good?
> You see, I have received His command to bless Israel. He has blessed, and I cannot reverse or qualify it. (Num. 23:8, 19–20)

What God says He will do regarding blessing and cursing, He will do. There is absolutely nothing a human being can do to reverse, change, alter, or nullify God's commandments. Neither can a human being do anything to impact the nature of God's promises.

God's commandments are absolutes. So are His promises of blessing that are associated with the keeping of His various statutes.

What God blesses, man cannot effectively curse.

What God curses, man cannot effectively bless.

Oh, we try as human beings to say that certain things are not a sin. We try to say that certain efforts we make are worthy of blessing although they have nothing to do with God's commandments. We try to justify our behavior in every way we can. It is to no avail.

The only choice we have is to obey or disobey. We can choose to line up our lives with God's Word, or we can choose to go our own way. In choosing our own way, of course, we are choosing to walk a way that is apart from God's blessing. To *choose* to be apart from God is to *choose* a way that is subject to God's judgment.

Moses admonished the Israelites:

You shall diligently keep the commandments of the Lord your God and His exhortations and His statutes which He commanded you.

And you shall do what is right and good in the sight of the Lord, that it may go well with you and that you may go in and possess the good land which the Lord swore to give to your fathers,

To cast out all your enemies from before you, as the Lord has promised. (Deut. 6:17–19)

Diligently Keep. The Israelites were commanded to *diligently* keep God's statues. In other words, they were to work faithfully at keeping them. At no time were they to wink at God's commandments or to take them lightly.

Keep All. In another place in the Law, Moses conveyed to the Israelites God's command that they were to keep *all* of His statutes and to remember all of His ways in providing for them as they had wandered in the wilderness. We read in Deuteronomy 8:1–2—

> All the commandments which I command you
> this day you shall be watchful to do, that you may
> live and multiply and go in and possess the land
> which the Lord swore to give to your fathers.
> And you shall [earnestly] remember all the
> way which the Lord your God led you these forty
> years in the wilderness, to humble you and to
> prove you.

No Substitutes. The Israelites certainly were not to substitute God's commandments for their own laws or the laws of any other god. The Israelites were admonished severely on this point:

> You shall make for yourselves no idols nor
> shall you erect a graven image, pillar, or obelisk,
> nor shall you place any figured stone in your land
> to which or on which to bow down; for I am the
> Lord your God.
> You shall keep My Sabbaths and reverence My
> sanctuary. I am the Lord. (Lev. 26:1–2)

Throughout God's Word, God's presence and God's blessings are linked to those who worship Him as the one true and living God, and who revere Him in both time and space—Sabbath and sanctuary.

The Link Between
Obedience and Increase

What was the reward to those who kept all of God's commandments with diligence? Moses gave this promise of God's provision and presence:

> If you walk in My statutes and keep My
> commandments and do them,
> I will give you rain in due season, and the land
> shall yield her increase and the trees of the field
> yield their fruit.

And your threshing [time] shall reach to the vintage and the vintage [time] shall reach to the sowing time, and you shall eat your bread to the full and dwell in your land securely.

I will give peace in the land; you shall lie down and none shall fill you with dread or make you afraid; and I will clear ferocious (wild) beasts out of the land, and no sword shall go through your land.

And you shall chase your enemies, and they shall fall before you by the sword.

Five of you shall chase a hundred, and a hundred of you shall put ten thousand to flight; your enemies shall fall before you by the sword.

For I will be leaning toward you with favor and regard for you, rendering you fruitful, multiplying you, and establishing and ratifying My covenant with you. (Lev. 26:3–9)

What a wonderful thing to know the Lord is leaning toward us with favor and regard—making us fruitful, multiplying us, and establishing and ratifying His covenant with us!

If you want to receive the fullness of God's increase in all areas of your life, there simply is no substitute for keeping the commandments of God fully and joyfully. You may not like some of God's commandments, but that doesn't change your requirement to obey them. You may wish you could compromise on some of

> *God's promise is that your "herds and flocks multiply and your silver and gold is multiplied and all you have is multiplied." (Deut. 8:13)*

God's rules—in the end, you cannot. God's fullness of increase for you lies in your keeping *all* His commandments, precepts, and statutes.

To those who keep all of God's commandments, God's

promise is that your "herds and flocks multiply and your silver and gold is multiplied and all you have is multiplied." (Deut. 8:13).

Note that phrase "all you have is multiplied." That includes not only the tangible expressions of your increase (in their case, flocks and herds—in our case, property and valuables) and the representational expressions of your increase (in their case, silver and gold—in our case, money, stocks, bonds, and other monetary vehicles)...it also includes all you have. *All* includes every aspect of your life—your creative ideas, physical health, emotional well-being, family relationships and friendships. *All!*

A Failure to Obey

What happens to those who fail to keep God's commandments?

A sobering story in the Book of Joshua portrays what happens when we do not follow God's commandments fully:

> But the Israelites committed a trespass in regard to the devoted things; for Achan son of Carmi, the son of Zabdi, the son of Zerah, of the tribe of Judah, took some of the things devoted [for destruction]. And the anger of the Lord burned against Israel.
>
> Joshua sent men from Jericho to Ai, which is near Beth-aven, east of Bethel, and said to them, Go up and spy out the land. So the men went up and spied out Ai.
>
> And they returned to Joshua and said to him, Let not all the men go up; but let about two thousand or three thousand go up and attack Ai; do not make the whole army toil up there, for they of Ai are few.
>
> So about three thousand Israelites went up there, but they fled before the men of Ai.
>
> And the men of Ai killed about thirty-six of them, for they chased them from before the gate

as far as Shebarim, and slew them at the descent. And the hearts of the people melted and became as water.

Then Joshua rent his clothes and lay on the earth upon his face before the ark of the Lord until evening, he and the elders of Israel; and they put dust on their heads. (Josh. 7:1–6)

Joshua cried out to the Lord, asking God why He had allowed this defeat of His people. The Lord replied, "Israel has sinned; they have transgressed My covenant which I commanded them." (Josh. 7:11) The Lord went on to state specifically how the people had sinned—they had disobeyed God's mandate that they destroy everything in Jericho with the exception of Rahab and her family and the gold, silver, bronze, and iron vessels which were put into the treasury of the Lord's house. Achan, however, had taken some items from Jericho in blatant disobedience—a mantel, two hundred shekels of silver, and a bar of gold weighing fifty shekels. He buried them in a hole he dug inside his tent.

The Lord said, "I will cease to be with you unless you destroy the accursed [devoted] things among you...You can not stand before your enemies until you take away from among you the things devoted [to destruction]." (Josh. 7:12–13)

None of us enjoys hearing about sin. We need to be reminded periodically, however, of its deadly consequences. The apostle Paul was clear, "For the wages which sin pays is death, but the [bountiful] free gift of God is eternal life through (in union with) Jesus Christ our Lord." (Rom. 6:23) Obedience brings great blessing.

Disobedience brings destruction and death.

No Middle Ground

God has only two categories for behaviors, attitudes, and things: blessed or accursed. There's no middle ground. The same goes for obedience. We either obey or disobey. We don't obey a little or disobey a little.

The Lord made a dramatic statement to Joshua in telling him *why* the Israelites have not been able to stand before their enemies: "They are accursed and have become devoted [for destruction]." (Josh. 7:12) In taking things that had been designated for destruction, and in making those things a part of their lives, the Israelites themselves became designated for destruction. Their possession of "accursed" items brought the curse of God on their own lives.

What a sobering word that should be to us. There are certain things that God does not want as part of our lives—they are things, practices, and affiliations that will destroy us. If we rebel against His commandments and take those cursed things into our lives and continue to hold on to them, God has no other choice but to watch us self-destruct. We have willfully chosen our own fate.

> *God has only two categories for*
> *behaviors, attitudes, and things:*
> *blessed or accursed.*

Does God desire for a person to use illegal drugs? Absolutely not. If a person willfully chooses to take illegal drugs, that person has pushed a self-destruct button. The cursed thing has brought a curse on the person.

Does God authorize a person to embezzle money from a company? Absolutely not. If a person willfully chooses to steal money, that person has put himself into a "cursed" position, subject to all the consequences that thievery can generate.

Does God plan and purpose for a person to have children out of wedlock? No. If a person willfully chooses to live a promiscuous life, that person puts himself into a position to reap the consequences of his behavior. Does God desire for a person to get AIDS through illicit sexual behavior? Absolutely not. But if a person willfully chooses to engage in fornication (sex apart from marriage) that person is putting himself into an accursed category.

When you put yourself into an accursed category by willfully associating with accursed things and practices, you do not enter that category alone. People talk about "private" sin, but no sin is ever private. Other people are always impacted or influenced in some way.

The truth is you become like those with whom you associate.

Achan's one-man, "private" sin affected all the Israelites. It brought about the death of thirty-six men. It put all of Israel into an accursed state before God. In the end, Achan's sin brought death to himself and to his children, his oxen, his donkeys, and his sheep. His tent and all that he had was burned.

Your sin will touch others. It will bring *decrease* upon them. In the end, if your sin remains unconfessed and unforgiven, it will destroy your life and all your possessions.

If Achan had not sinned in Jericho, he would have been greatly blessed at the eventual defeat of Ai. After God's judgment upon Achan and his family, the Lord said to Joshua, "Arise, go up to Ai...and you shall do to Ai and its king as you did to Jericho and its king, except that its spoil and its cattle [this time] you shall take as booty for yourselves." (Josh. 8:1-2) Achan could have brought home great possessions from Ai if he had only been willing to do things God's way rather than his own way.

Does God expect such strict adherence to His commandments in New Testament times? Definitely.

The apostle Paul wrote to the Corinthians:

> It is actually reported that there is sexual immorality among you, impurity of a sort that is condemned and does not occur even among the heathen; for a man has [his own] father's wife....
>
> You are to deliver this man over to Satan for physical discipline [to destroy carnal lusts which prompted him to incest], that [his] spirit may [yet] be saved in the day of the Lord Jesus.

...Do you not know that [just a little leaven will ferment the whole lump [of dough]?" (I Cor. 5:1, 5–6)

The sin of this one man created a negative situation for the entire church at Corinth. Paul went on to admonish the church not to habitually associate with anyone who called himself a Christian but who was also known to be immoral, greedy, an idolater, a person with a foul tongue, a drunkard, a swindler, or a robber. (See I Cor. 5:11.) He was not saying they should shun such people or that they should refrain from sharing the Gospel with such people—he said they were not to *associate* with them. The truth is you become like those with whom you associate. We are never to bind our lives or to enter into covenant relationships with unbelievers. (See II Cor. 6:14.)

When it comes to the increase of our life, we cannot force the hand of God, but we can bind the hand of God. Our human will cannot require anything of God, but with our human will, we can limit the work of God. God will not overstep the bounds of our human will. We must *choose* to obey His commandments. We must *choose* to put ourselves into the position where He can increase us in righteousness, purity, virtue, and holiness. Only then can we experience *whole-life increase.*

I encourage you today: Choose to obey God. Choose to do things His way. Your obedience is a pre-requisite for your increase.

Chapter 5

Our Part in Acting on God's Promises: Fruitfulness

Have you ever wondered what God desires for you to do on this earth?

The answer is this: You are to be *fruitful.*

From the very beginning, God has commanded us as men and women to be *fruitful.* The first thing God said to the first man and woman was this: "Be fruitful, multiply, and fill the earth, and subdue it [using all its vast resources in the service of God and man]." (Gen. 1:28)

Many people desire to multiply and be blessed without being fruitful. To be fruitful requires that a person do something—to be fruitful a person must plan, cultivate, and harvest. In Genesis 26:22 we find Isaac saying, "The Lord has made room for us, and we shall be fruitful in the land." The Lord will make "room" for us—give us a place and an opportunity—but we must be fruitful.

The apostle Paul wrote to the Colossians after Epaphras had informed him of their great love in the Holy Spirit:

> For this reason we also, from the day we heard of it, have not ceased to pray and make [special] request for you, [asking] that you may be filled with the full (deep and clear) knowledge of His

will in all spiritual wisdom [in comprehensive insight into the ways and purposes of God] and in understanding and discernment of spiritual things—

That you may walk (live and conduct yourselves) in a manner worthy of the Lord, fully pleasing to Him and desiring to please Him in all things, bearing fruit in every good work and steadily growing and increasing in and by the knowledge of God [with fuller, deeper, and clearer insight, acquaintance, and recognition]. (Col. 1:9–10)

Fruitfulness is not something that happens overnight. It is not something that happens only once in life. Fruitfulness is the very tenor of life. It is the natural and normal by-product of the Christian who is intent on daily walking out God's plan and purpose—living out the every-day routines and responsibilities of life without becoming bogged down in them.

There are those who claim that the first step a person takes toward a goal is the most difficult step. Others claim that the last step across the finish line is the most difficult. My contention is that there is a certain exhilaration and energy that is associated with launching out on a new project. There is also a certain momentum that seems to carry us across the finish line at the end, giving us an extra boost of energy. The most difficult steps are the steps in between the first and last! That's where we face the mundane daily chores and responsibilities.

The craving of youthful ambition is to do some great thing or experience some great miracle. To do quiet duty honestly...to walk in steadfast commitment to the Lord...to cling to hope and to look for the fulfillment of God's promises....to walk out the *life* of Christ...is what truly satisfies the mature heart as the years come and go.

Every Good Work

Fruitfulness occurs as we *use* the talents God has given us. Every person has a gift—a talent, an innate ability, a God-given trait or capacity—that can provide benefit to others. I believe a person can determine his gift primarily by knowing what he hates and what he loves. The more a person knows what he enjoys doing and what he doesn't enjoy doing, the more focused he is going to be in understanding his gifts from God. A number of tests are available, as well, to help a person discover his giftedness.

Any time a person attempts to work outside his gift, he is going to feel uncomfortable, ill at ease, or miserable. It is only when a person works within his gift that he truly feels fulfilled and purposeful.

A person who is gifted to work with children will feel most comfortable, blessed, and fulfilled in working with children—he won't feel that way working with adults. A person who is gifted to be a helper behind the scenes isn't going to feel comfortable on stage.

You may be able to succeed to some degree as you function in gifts that aren't yours, but your greatest success is going to come as you work *within* the gifts God has given you. He has designed you to fill a unique role in His plan for the ages, and He has given you all the gifts you need in order to do what He has called you to do.

Our job is to develop our gifts and to acquire all of the skills necessary to employ our gifts to their fullest. For example, a person might be gifted in music. What is required of that person? Practice, and more practice. The person gifted in music will *enjoy* practicing, delight in learning how to read music, and enjoy developing his voice or his skills in playing a particular instrument. The more skilled the person becomes, the greater the opportunities to express the gift.

What do your gifts require of you? They require you to learn all you can to express your gifts to the best of your ability. They require you to develop the skills associated with your gifts. They require you to grow in your *use* of the gifts. At every stage of developing your gifts, you should be using them.

I once heard a recording artist say, "The critics are calling me an overnight wonder. Yeah, right. I've been playing and singing for twenty years in small clubs and county fairs and charity events. I've sung back-up and been part of singing groups since I was eight years old. There's nothing 'overnight' about me. It's only the spotlight of public attention and success that has suddenly fallen on me. For a long time, I've been singing the songs as well as I sing them now."

The timing of God's "spotlight" on your life is not something you can predict. What you *can* do is prepare your gifts and prepare your heart so you are in a position to "shine" when that spotlight falls on you.

I have worked hard all my life. I'm not bragging or complaining. Work is *supposed* to be part of life. I started working at age ten, throwing newspapers and mowing lawns. I went to work part-time at the mill when I was fourteen and by the time I was sixteen, I went to school full-time and worked a full shift at the mill.

I drove a bus and worked as a janitor to help pay my bills when I was in Bible college. After college, my wife and I moved to Toledo to take over a small church with forty-five adults. We worked hard and preached faithfully and did our best to love the people generously. Over a twenty-year period, that church grew to more than two thousand people and I have had opportunities to preach around the world.

Has God increased my life? Absolutely!

Did that increase happen overnight? No.

Did that increase happen without work? No.

Trusting God for Fruit

Work alone, of course, does not create fruitfulness. No farmer can force a plant to grow fruit. A farmer can work the orchard and do all the right things that create an environment in which fruitfulness can occur, but no farmer can *cause* fruit to come from a tree. Only God can *cause* anything—plant, human being, or church—to be fruitful.

We must never lose sight of the fact that we are to trust God to bring about fruit from our labor. We are to do our part—develop our gifts and use them—and then trust God to do His part.

Greater Effectiveness and Productivity. One thing I've discovered through personal experience over the years is that when I try to employ any of my gifts *without* total trust on the Lord, I make mistakes and I get tired. In sharp contrast, when I employ my gifts *with* great trust in the Lord, I am much more productive and effective and accurate in hitting the targets God places before me.

Less Worry and Stress. Furthermore, I do not get weary when I trust God fully as I work. That doesn't mean I don't get physically tired at times, but I do not get "weary." I do not feel frantic or stressed out. I do not become discouraged at little problems and obstacles that fall into my path. Rather, I feel an exhilaration and an energy that is accompanied by a deep joy at knowing that I have been used by God and that God is well-pleased at my heart's motives and my willingness to obey Him.

In Ephesians 3:20, the apostle Paul wrote, "Now to Him Who, by (in consequence of) the [action of His] power that is at work within us, is able to [carry out His purpose and] do superabundantly, far over and above all that we [dare] ask or think [infinitely beyond our highest prayers, desires, thoughts, hopes, or dreams]."

Superabundantly, far and above all that we dare ask or think! Talk about increase! Most of us can imagine a great deal—we have secret thoughts, hopes, dreams, and desires that are far-

---

Has God increased my life? Absolutely!
Did that increase happen overnight? No.
Did that increase happen without work? No.

---

reaching. Yet God's Word tells us that God has all that and more for us.

But there's a condition established in this powerful Word about God's increase: *In consequence of the action of His power that is at work within us.* We will receive a superabundant increase only to the extent that we allow God's power to be at work in us.

How is the extent of His power in us determined? By the degree of our commitment to the Lord and our trust in Him.

God's work in us is directly related to the degree we surrender or submit our lives to Him. The more we trust God to work all things to our eternal benefit and work through us to help others around us, the greater our commitment to allow Him to work in us. If we are only willing to submit one small area of our life to Him, He will work in that one small area. If we are willing to surrender all that we have, are, and will ever be, He will work in the totality of our life. He will produce *whole-life increase.*

I encourage you today: Be fruitful! Work hard at developing your God-given abilities. Work hard in using your talents and skills. And then, trust God to bring forth fruit from your life.

Chapter 6

Our Part in Acting on God's Promises: Giving

One of the most important areas of obedience in any Christian's life is the area of giving. To receive in abundance, one must *first* give faithfully and generously. The laws of planting and reaping are universal—what we sow, we reap.

Two key principles are involved in sowing and reaping:

- The *quantity* of seed we sow is related to the quantity we reap—more seed planted, more harvest reaped.
- The *quality* of the seed we sow is related to the goodness and quality of the harvest we reap—good seed bears good fruit.

The apostle Paul wrote to the Galatians, "Do not be deceived and deluded and misled; God will not allow Himself to be sneered at (scorned, disdained, or mocked by mere pretensions or professions, or by His precepts being set aside). [He inevitably deludes himself who attempts to delude God.] For whatever a man sows, that and that only is what he will reap." (Gal. 6:7)

The Lavish Response of God

One of the most amazing stories about giving and receiving and about increase is found in I Kings 10. It involves a woman we have come to call the queen of Sheba.

This woman "heard of [the constant connection of] the fame of Solomon with the name of the Lord." (I Kings 10:1) What she heard compelled her to act. She traveled to Jerusalem with a great camel train bearing spices, gold, and precious stones. She came to Solomon to ask him the questions that were burning in her heart.

The queen of Sheba ate at King Solomon's table, and after she had been given a royal tour and she had seen all the wealth of his household and the Temple, she said,

> It was a true report I heard in my own land of your acts and sayings and wisdom.
>
> I did not believe it until I came and my eyes had seen. Behold, the half was not told me. You have added wisdom and goodness exceeding the fame I heard.
>
> Happy are your men! Happy are these your servants who stand continually before you, hearing your wisdom!
>
> Blessed be the Lord your God, Who delighted in you and set you on the throne of Israel! Because the Lord loved Israel forever, He made you king to execute justice and righteousness. (I Kings 10:6–9)

Solomon's Temple has been estimated at a value of $200 billion in today's money. That amount of money is so vast it boggles the mind! Solomon's palace was also opulent. Certainly there was a great deal to be bring about awe and amazement in this queen. The queen even took note of the apparel and attitude of Solomon's servants.

As an important part of the protocol related to her visit, she gave Solomon expensive, elaborate gifts. In return, he "gave to the queen of Sheba all she wanted, whatever she asked, besides his gifts to her from his royal bounty." (I Kings 10:13) She received in return *far more than she had given.*

The queen of Sheba received gifts from the royal treasury. In addition, she received "whatever she asked." And finally, she received "all she wanted."

The gifts from the royal treasury were customary gifts. A person coming to visit a king brought unique gifts from his or her nation—spices and perfumes, birds and animals, and other items that were distinctive and unusual. In return, the custom of courts in that time called for the hosting monarch to give gifts unique to his nation and to give back slightly more in value than what had been given. The queen of Sheba may have given Solomon ten million dollars worth of gifts—from the royal treasury alone she likely received back eleven or twelve million dollars in gifts. But then...look at the additional gifts she received!

She received all that she asked. Solomon did not withhold from her anything that she requested. He had given her a full tour of his royal home and grounds. In that part of the world, a compliment about a particular item very often resulted in that item being *given* to the person. It could very well be that all the queen of Sheba noted with a compliment was given to her as a present.

She received all that she wanted. Solomon went beyond what the queen complimented or requested. He saw those things that she *desired* and he gave her what he knew she secretly wanted in her heart but had not voiced with her lips.

In addition to all of the material wealth bestowed upon her, she received even greater riches in the form of *wisdom.* In having her questions answered, she truly received "all that she wanted."

What a picture of the way God meets our needs with His increase!

How Do You Approach God, Our King?

Let's look a little closer at this queen's amazing journey. The queen of Sheba traveled by camel about fifteen hundred miles from her home to Jerusalem. No matter how much luxury may have been lavished upon her enroute, this trip was still an extremely long and difficult one. She was willing to risk her life and a sizable amount of wealth to make this journey. What motivated her to make such a journey?

A Hunger for God. Bible historians tell us that part of her mission may have been to secure favor along the trade route guarded by Solomon's soldiers. The Bible itself tells us that this queen came to Solomon *hungry* for insight into what made him great. She not only wanted to know the man but to know the source of the man's power and wealth. She knew that his fame was linked with the name of the Lord, and she came to probe his relationship with God and the nature of the God that Solomon served.

A Willingness to Give. This queen came *willing to give* of what she had. She gave of her time to make this journey. She gave of her wealth. She came with open hands, as well as an open mind and an open heart.

An Attitude of Praise. This queen came with an *attitude of praise*. She did not express envy to Solomon, rather she expressed great admiration. She blessed the Lord God. She recognized that God had given Solomon wisdom and the ability to govern Israel with justice and righteousness. She stated that no report of Solomon had been exaggerated—nothing about him and his reign disappointed her or fell short of her expectations. He exceeded her greatest imagination.

These three hallmarks of her journey—a hunger for God, a willingness to give, and an attitude of praise—are the way God desires for us to come to Him. He longs for us to make the effort to search out the hidden riches of His Word, to discover *all* that He has for us, and to acknowledge all that He is and will forever be.

The queen of Sheba was not disappointed. Her desire for the wisdom of God was met. Her desire to meet and to know the King was met. And as she returned home, she returned home *increased* by her journey, not decreased.

She went home rich in wisdom, rich in relationship, rich in experience, rich in faith, and rich in material wealth. Every aspect of her life had been blessed and multiplied.

Far more than Solomon gave to the queen of Sheba, Jesus has that much and more to give to you. Jesus said with reference to Himself, "The queen of the South will arise in the judgment with the people of this age and generation and condemn them; for she came from the ends of the [inhabited] earth to listen to the wisdom of Solomon, and notice, here is more than Solomon." (Luke 11:31)

When you come to the King of Kings, He is going to satisfy your longings for wisdom, knowledge, and understanding. He is going to meet your desires and needs. He is going to far exceed your greatest ideas and imaginations when it comes to His glory and majesty. He is going to make your deepest and most noble dreams come true. And more!

We Are Commanded to Give

Giving for the queen of Sheba was voluntary. God, however, *commands* His people to give. Giving is considered to be vitally important for God's people. Why? Because giving is a key that helps to unlock the riches of God's storehouse.

A sobering yet hopeful Word of the Lord was given to the prophet Malachi:

> For I am the Lord, I do not change; that is why you, O sons of Jacob, are not consumed.
>
> Even from the days of your fathers you have turned aside from My ordinances and have not kept them. Return to me, and I will return to you, says the Lord of hosts. But you say, How shall we return?
>
> Will a man rob or defraud God? Yet you rob and defraud Me. But you say, In what way do we rob or defraud You? [You have withheld your] tithes and offerings.

You are cursed with the curse, for you are
robbing Me, even this whole nation.

Bring all the tithes (the whole tenth of your
income) into the storehouse, that there may be food
in My house, and prove Me now by it, says the
Lord of hosts, if I will not open the windows of
heaven for you and pour you out a blessing, that
there shall not be room enough to receive it.

And I will rebuke the devourer [insects and
plagues] for your sakes and he shall not destroy
the fruits of your ground, neither shall your vine
drop its fruit before the time in the field, says the
Lord of hosts.

And all nations shall call you happy and
blessed, for you shall be a land of delight, says the
Lord of hosts. (Mal. 3:6–12)

The Lord accurately and rightly accused the Israelites of
robbing Him. This word "rob" actually means to conceal
goodness—to keep people from partaking or experiencing the
goodness of God. It's a term similar to the one used for covering
a full goblet of wine with a cloth. To "rob" someone means to
keep that person from partaking of the good things a "host" desires
for them to receive.

The Israelites had, through their disobedience regarding
giving, kept God from pouring out His life-giving and enriching
presence into their lives. They had robbed God from the pleasure
of pouring out a blessing. They had thwarted His desire. Their
sin had kept His blessing concealed and locked up in heaven.

Those who fail to give as God commands do the same thing
today. They "rob" God of pouring out a blessing. To fail to give
according to what God requires is to "lock up" a blessing that
God desires to give but cannot give because of man's disobedience.

God's standard is the tithe—ten percent. That standard is
fixed. It has never been changed throughout the millennia of
God's law. It is just as much the standard today as it ever was.

My advice to you is very simple: You need to keep giving to God regardless of other circumstances in your life. Never stop tithing.

If all Christians would give their tithe, the church would never have a need for money. Local evangelism efforts and outreach programs to the needy would soar. More missionaries could be sent to areas of the world that still must be reached for Christ. The Gospel could be beamed into every dark corner of this world.

And all along the way, God's people would be blessed with an increase of overflowing proportions. Those in the church would be blessed beyond their imagining!

The Sin of Self-Indulgence

We are a nation of consumers, and the fact is we are a nation of self-indulgent consumption. We spend more on *ourselves* than any people on earth. We have more luxury items per capita, more clothing per capita, more jewelry per capita, and more television sets and more automobiles per capita than any nation. The average "poor" person in our land lives with a better set of possessions than the average "upper middle class" person in most third-world countries!

To be self-indulgent means simply that a person thinks first and foremost about spending what he earns on himself. For most wage earners, taxes are deducted from their paycheck even before the check reaches the worker's hands. The worker then holds his paycheck in his hands and says, "All mine. I can spend this however I choose."

The prudent put a little in savings or retirement investments—again, for the benefit of self. The person who is conscientious in caring for his family makes sure that housing, food, and utility bills are paid. But then what? Most people assume that the rest of the check is for spending in whatever way they desire—and generally on things that gratify *self.*

From God's standpoint, the tithe is supposed to come off the "top" of one's earnings. It is supposed to be the *first fruits* of what one acquires. That first dime of every dollar earned is intended to be put into God's storehouse to be used for the work of the Lord.

Why did God require this of His people? For their *benefit*. The number "ten" in the Bible has a unique meaning. It stands for commandments or law, such as the Ten Commandments, but it also stands for *increase*. The tithe was God's law related to their *increase*. The basic line of reasoning is this: If a person keeps God's law, he will be increased in every area of his life. The person who gives to God's storehouse the tithe of his earnings is putting himself into obedience when it comes to his fruitfulness. The result is *increase*.

In our natural thinking, we see giving a tenth of what we receive as diminishing our income. From God's perspective, that tenth becomes a seed for an eventual harvest of multiplication. The tithe becomes the key to increase. In truth, tithing is God's *pre-requisite* to your receiving His full blessing on your life.

You may be saying, "Do you mean to tell me that if I don't tithe, God won't bless me?"

Hear it from God's Word. God said through Malachi to those who had stopped tithing: "You are cursed with the curse, for you are robbing Me, even this whole nation." (Mal. 3:9) What is cursed cannot be blessed!

The Turn-Around of a Nation

One of the greatest stories in the Bible about increase involves a turn-around in an entire nation. It is the story of Hezekiah's reign. (See II Chron. 29–32.)

At the outset of Hezekiah's reign, the doors of the Temple were closed. Hezekiah re-opened them and set in order the full worship protocol of the Temple. He encouraged the Levites to purify themselves, to resume their duties and to cleanse the Temple and all its vessels. He restored songs of praise to the Temple, with the singers accompanied by the trumpets and other instruments ordained by King David. The king himself bowed and worshiped before the Lord and ordered that the entire assembly bring sacrifices and thank offerings.

Then Hezekiah ordered that the Passover feast be kept for the first time in many years. He called on people throughout the land to come up to Jerusalem and many responded. Hezekiah prayed, asking God to pardon all who came and "the Lord hearkened to Hezekiah and healed the people." (II Chron. 30:20)

When the people returned home, they overthrew all of the symbols of idolatry in their cities and in the "high places." Praise began to flow through the land and so did giving. Hezekiah commanded the people to give the portion due the priests and Levites and "as soon as the command went abroad, the Israelites gave in abundance the firstfruits of grain, vintage fruit, oil, honey, and of all the produce of the field; and they brought in abundantly the tithe of everything." (II Chron. 31:5) Within a very short time, the Bible tells us there were "heaps" of offerings in the Temple and chambers were built to store the overflow.

Was Israel reduced by this giving? Far from it! The Lord supernaturally defeated Sennacherib, the king of Assyria, who had invaded Judah. This Assyrian king had insulted God's people and God Himself. He had terrorized the people of Jerusalem after putting the city under siege. When Hezekiah and the prophet Isaiah prayed and cried to heaven, the "Lord sent an angel, who cut off all the mighty warriors and commanders and officers in the camp of the king of Assyria. So the Assyrian king returned with shamed face to his own land. And when he came into the house of his god, they who were his own offspring slew him there with the sword." (II Chron. 32:21) The Israelites were spared from the ruthless power of Assyria. They prospered and were guided by the Lord in all they did.

Personally, Hezekiah prospered as king. The Bible tells us that "every work that he began in the service of the house of God, in keeping with the law and the commandments to seek his God [inquiring of and yearning for Him], he did with all his heart, and he prospered." (II Chron. 31:21) He had "very great wealth and honor and he made for himself treasuries for silver, gold, precious stones, spices, shields, and all kinds of attractive vessels." (II Chron. 32:27) He also built storehouses for the abundant amounts of grain, vintage fruits, oil, and animals that were given to him. The Bible tells us in a great summary statement that Hezekiah "prospered in all his works." (II Chron. 32:30) In fact, his reputation was so great that the princes of Babylon more than a thousand miles away began to inquire about the great increase of Israel.

Hezekiah *first* took care of the Temple and the things of God. *Then* he increased in his life. The same for the Israelites—they *first* brought their tithes to Jerusalem and *then* they increased.

The Principles of Giving
Are Still Valid Today

What God required in the past, He still requires today.

What God did in the past to increase people as a consequence of their giving, He still does today!

What is it that God is requiring of you today?

Will you be obedient in responding to His commandments regarding giving? Your increase lies in the balances of your answer.

I encourage you today: Obey God in your giving.

Chapter 7

Giving and Increase—
The Bigger Picture

There are several key principles for giving that are often overlooked by those who preach or teach about financial prosperity and success. They are principles vital to experiencing whole-life increase—indeed, they are principles that are vital for developing a genuine, trusting relationship with God.

Principle #1: We Are
Called to Give Our Selves

Most prosperity teachers only ask for people to give money. They desire nothing else from their "partners" or "ministry associates."

The Bible insists that for us to experience genuine increase, we must give our *selves.* Granted, money is a representation of self and it certainly must be included in our giving. As we discussed in the last chapter, the exact amount of the tithe is very specific.

The "big picture" about giving, however, calls for us to give far more than money or material possessions. We are to make available to the Lord *all* that we have—our time, our personalities, our natural abilities, our skills, our smiles, our hugs, our words of encouragement, our presence in times of need, our service, our praise and worship, our *lives.*

The apostle Paul wrote to the Romans, "I appeal to you therefore, brethren, and beg of you in view of [all] the mercies of God, to make a decisive dedication of your bodies [presenting all your members and faculties] as a living sacrifice, holy (devoted, consecrated) and well pleasing to God, which is your reasonable (rational, intelligent) service and spiritual worship." (Rom. 12:1)

Your prosperity is dependent upon how much you release your gifts into the Kingdom of God. Your gifts include your natural talents, your spiritual gifts, and your material resources. It is as you give "unto the Lord" that you put yourself into a position for life increase.

We are to hold back nothing that we are or have.

Not only are we to give of what we have personally, but we are to be conduits for what the Holy Spirit desires to give to the Body of Christ. The Scriptures make it very clear that when we come together as believers, we are to come prepared to speak to one another in psalms and hymns and spiritual songs, offering praise with our voice with thanksgiving in our hearts. (See Eph. 5:19 and Col. 3:16.)

All of the gifts of the Holy Spirit are intended to bring increase to the Body of Christ. They are for the "building up" of the believers so that *all* in the church might come to the full maturity of Christ Jesus.

The Holy Spirit at all times sees the lack that may exist in any one individual within a body of believers. He desires to see that need met and He knows precisely who has the "excess" to give to that person. As excess is given to those who lack, all others who experience the giving and the receiving are blessed. An overflow of anointing is generated that meets *all* needs and builds up the Body.

Your Gifts Make Room for You. Proverbs 18:16 tells us, "A man's gift makes room for him and brings him before great men." The more you give of the gifts God has given you, the greater the opportunities you will have to give your gifts. Your gifts are enlarged by use. In turn, your gifts will gain greater and greater notoriety as they are used.

A number of years ago at Ohio State University, the football team had a quarterback named Tom Matte. When Matte went to the pros, he played as a halfback for the Baltimore Colts. Then came the season when his team's quarterback became injured, and then the second-string quarterback went down. The coaches were at a loss as to who might fill the quarterback position. Then one of them said, "What about Tom Matte?"

Matte stepped into the position and guided the Colts to several victories. He had a "gifting" that nobody had fully recognized in the pro-football ranks. What Matte *had* done through the years, however, was *think* like a quarterback even as he *played* halfback. He knew all the plays, at times better than the quarterback. He knew how each member on the team was supposed to move for any given play, including the moves of the quarterback. He was ready mentally and physically to step into the role when the time came.

That is how we are to function as well. We are to train ourselves mentally and spiritually so that we are ready at any instance to respond under the direction of the Holy Spirit. We are to know the Scriptures and have them embedded in our memory. We are to pray for sensitivity, discernment, and guidance—and have practice in responding instantly to the direction of the Holy Spirit in our daily lives.

What you embed in your spirit will eventually have an opportunity to play out. The giving of your gifts creates room for the Holy Spirit to do His work in your life and in the lives of others. Your giftedness in the spiritual realm *will* find expression and manifestation. Trust the Holy Spirit to bring about the opportunity.

Principle #2: Our Harvest
Is Far More Than Economic

Most prosperity teachers tell their followers to look for a material, natural, physical, or financial harvest. They advocate a simple formula: "Give money, get money."

God's plan for whole-life increase is based on a different premise: "Give your entire life, get back an abundant life."

The Bible does *not* promise us that God will multiply every seed we plant in the form of material possessions that we can consume to fulfill our own greed or self-centered desires for recognition, reward, or self-esteem. God does not promise us an abundance of *stuff* so we might satisfy our own flesh. When He sends a harvest to us, He intends for that harvest to meet *all* the needs of our life—many of which are not financial or material. And, He intends for us to replant part of that harvest back into the soil of His Kingdom and to use the *overflow* of what we receive to extend the Gospel.

God knows what we *need* far more than we know what we need. He seeks to meet our *needs*, and our foremost need in life is to know Him. If we have not received Jesus Christ as our Savior, that is the foremost need in our life. If we have received Jesus Christ, then our foremost need is to know Him better and to grow to become more like Him. All other needs are secondary.

Certainly we have a need for food, shelter, and clothing. We have a need for health, energy, stamina, emotional well-being, friendship, and love. We have a need for hope and a sense of purpose and fulfillment in life.

Few people *need* a bigger house, an airplane, five cars, a fur coat, and a yacht! God does not cater to our excessive, self-focused desires for possessions. He longs for fellowship with us and for us to desire the things *He* desires on this earth—that more people might know Him and love Him, that the basic needs of all people might be met, and that people might live in hope and faith rather than in discouragement and fear.

Principle #3: Our Giving and Receiving Creates a "Balance" in the Body of Christ

Many prosperity teachers encourage people to give so they might receive a supply to meet their individual needs.

Genuine Bible-based increase admonishes people to give so that *all* within the Body of Christ might have sufficient supply.

I do not believe there is a church on the face of the earth that fully practices the intent of God for His church.

Some who are part of the church do not understand the principles necessary for giving and receiving. Some do not know what it is that they have to give—they are unaware of their natural and spiritual gifts or the fullness of the resources that are theirs to give. Some are reluctant to release their talents, resources, and time. Nevertheless, it is God's desire to bless ALL His people with increase and He has clearly set forth the principles and guidelines for bringing about increase. Those principles are deeply embedded in a mutual, freely-offered, joyously-rendered giving of one's talents, resources, and time *to the Body of Christ*, with a willingness to receive what others give of their talents, resources, and time.

Read these encouraging words from the apostle Paul to the Corinthian church:

> For if the [eager] readiness to give is there, then it is acceptable and welcomed in proportion to what a person has, not according to what he does not have,
> For it is not [intended] that other people be eased and relieved [of their responsibility] and you be burdened and suffer [unfairly],
> But to have equality [share and share alike], your surplus over necessity at the present time going to meet their want and to equalize the difference created by it, so that [at some other time] their surplus in turn may be given to supply your want. Thus there may be equality,
> As it is written, He who gathered much had nothing over, and he who gathered little did not lack. (II Cor. 8:12–15; see also Exod. 16:18)

We all know that there are times in which we seem to have more in the way of material or financial resources than at other times. We also have seasons in our lives when we seem to be able to volunteer more of our time. In like manner, we have seasons in our lives when our gifts seem to be flourishing and developing to the overflow point—we are more productive, more creative, and more efficient than at other times.

At whatever time or season we may be, we are to give generously from what we have that is beyond our need so that others may be blessed. In that way, we put ourselves into position for further personal increase, and we also bless the Body of Christ and "increase" the whole of the church.

Principle #4: Tithing Puts Us on Equal Footing for Increase

The Lord certainly does not ask us to give what we do not have—rather, to give of what we *do* have. Every person is commanded by God to give *in proportion* to the gifts and resources he has. That proportion is the tenth, or the tithe. Both rich and poor are to give in the same proportion.

Beyond the tithe, we are to give offerings out of the "overflow" of our lives.

Every person knows that when it comes to both farming and banking, one of the cardinal rules is this: If you put nothing in, you have no right to take anything out.

God's universe operates on a "seed" principle. What you plant is what you reap.

When it comes to the *quantity* of seed God asks us to plant, many people are confused. They believe that if a person gives a tithe of one hundred thousand dollars on a million-dollar income, that person has given more than the person who gives a thousand dollars on a ten-thousand-dollar income. Not so from God's perspective. Both the millionaire and the ten-thousand-dollar person have given a tithe. They are on equal footing before God. Their faithfulness to tithing puts them automatically into a category of "obedience" before the Lord. Both are in position to receive God's increase.

Jesus gave a parable about this very principle in Matthew 25:14–46. In this parable, Jesus told about a man who planned to take a long journey and he called three servants and entrusted his property to them. To one he gave five talents, to another two talents, and to the third a single talent. When the man returned he found that the servant given five talents had doubled the talents. So had the servant who was given two talents. To each of these servants, the master said, "Well done, you upright (honorable, admirable) and faithful servant! You have been faithful and trustworthy over a little; I will put you in charge of much. Enter into and share the joy (the delight, the blessedness) which your master enjoys." (See Matt. 25:23.)

The master did not differentiate the reward for these servants, even though one had doubled five talents to ten and the other two talents to four. The fact was that each servant had invested the talents and doubled them.

God does not look at specific numbers—He looks at the *portion* or the *state* of our giving. He looks at the tithe, not the dollar sign associated with the tithe. He looks at the investment or the use of a talent for the furtherance of His Kingdom, not the specific kind of talent or the value of that talent in the eyes of men.

This is a critically important point. God sees our motives, our intent, our desires in giving...He sees our faithfulness in giving...He sees the relationship between what we give to Him and what we keep for ourselves...and He blesses those who give sacrificially, generously, joyfully, and in faith.

Jesus watched a widow give two mites (less than a penny) into the offering coffers of the Temple and said she had given more than the rich He had watched that day. Why? Not because her offering was greater in amount, but because she gave sacrificially out of her need, while they gave simply out of their excess. She had given her all to the Lord, trusting Him fully to meet her needs. Those who had given much larger offerings, monetarily speaking, had given to be seen and acknowledged as rich by others who observed their giving. (See Luke 21:2–4.)

In many ways, my mother was like that widow who gave two mites. Mom got paid on Thursdays and within an hour after she arrived home on payday, her check was cashed, she had paid the insurance man, and she had tucked a tithe of her income into her Bible to give as the offering plate was passed on Sunday. Mom tithed in good times and bad. By her giving, she "obligated" God to take care of us—to be the Source of our provision, protection, and power. She put herself and her family into a position to receive God's promised blessings, no matter the circumstances that might be swirling around us.

Why am I making such a point of this? Because many people seem to give with an attitude, *Hey, I gave a thousand dollars to God's work—isn't that enough?* No, it isn't enough if it isn't a tithe of what you have been given by God. God's standard is the tithe. That is the basic requirement. Offerings are above and beyond the tithe.

Principle #5: We Are To Give Prayerfully and with Faith

Rarely have I heard a prosperity teacher talk about the role of prayer when it comes to increase. All too often, they limit their teaching to "seed in, harvest out."

Just as water and fertilizer are vital to the growth of a seed into a fruitful plant, so prayer and faith are vital to the progression of increase in our lives. All of our giving should be accompanied by prayer and should be rooted in faith.

Cornelius was a man who both prayed to God and gave alms to men consistently. He was faithful in his worship and his giving. The angel of the Lord appeared to him one afternoon and said, "Your prayers and your [generous] gifts to the poor have come up [as a sacrifice] to God and have been remembered by Him." (Acts 10:4) Cornelius was instructed by the angel to send for Simon Peter, which he did. The result was not only the salvation of Cornelius and his entire household, but the opening of the Gospel to the entire Gentile world! (See Acts 10.)

Cornelius' *praying and giving* opened a door and created the way for him to hear the Gospel and accept Jesus as his Savior. His *praying and giving* opened the door to his having a relationship with Peter. His *praying and giving* opened the door to the salvation of his household and, ultimately, to a great, uncountable multitude of people through the ages.

As You Give, Ask God to Meet Your Needs. Be bold in asking God to meet your needs. Jesus told a parable about an insistent widow who came again and again to a judge to receive justice. He told this story to teach that we "ought always to pray and not to turn coward (faint, lose heart, and give up)." (Luke 18:1) In other words, we are to pray continually with courageous faith.

I am a deeply passionate person. I don't live my life in the abstract. I *feel* my life. I want my life to make a difference. I don't want to be a by-stander—I am an active participant in life. And when it comes to prayer, I choose to be aggressive in my faith. I want to believe God for *all* that He has for me.

How aggressive is your faith today? The apostle Paul said to the Ephesians that God desires to provide for them far over and above all that we *dare* ask or think. To *dare* is to be aggressive in our asking in faith.

James 1:6–7 tells us, "Only it must be in faith that he asks with no wavering (no hesitating, no doubting). For the one who wavers (hesitates, doubts) is like the billowing surge out at sea that is blown hither and thither and tossed by the wind. For truly, let not such a person imagine that he will receive anything [he asks for] from the Lord."

Principle #6: We Must
Release Our Gifts to Excellence

Your increase is dependent in part upon the degree to which you release your gifts to *excellence*. Just as a planted seed sprouts and must then be cultivated...so your natural talents need to be developed, your spiritual gifts need to be exercised, and your material gifts need to be given to the best of your ability. All must be given as if you are personally presenting your gifts directly into the hands of the Lord Jesus.

God desires that we bring to Him gifts and offerings that are "without blemish." (See Lev. 1:10; 3:1; 3:6 as examples.) This means that we bring to God that which is without sin, compromise, or self-justification. Nothing we give should fall into the "second best" or "left-overs" category.

No Israelite was to bring a sick, maimed, or dead animal for a sacrifice. As a part of the prophetic utterance of Malachi, we learn that the Israelites were also guilty of bringing polluted food and maimed animals to the Temple for sacrifice. The Lord spoke through the prophet, "When you [priests] offer blind [animals] for sacrifice, is it not evil? And when you offer the lame and the sick, is it not evil? Present such a thing [a blind or lame or sick animal] now to your governor [in payment of your taxes, and see what will happen]. Will he be pleased with you? Or will he receive you graciously? says the Lord of hosts." (Mal. 1:8)

Not only were the Israelites bringing animals and offerings that were blemished, they were lackluster in their worship. Malachi gave this Word from the Lord: "You say also, Behold, what a drudgery and weariness this is! And you have sniffed at it, says the Lord of hosts." (Mal. 1:13)

Any time we come before the Lord, we must come with our best energy, our best focus, and our best attitude. As a pastor, I am amazed at the number of people who cannot stand for twenty minutes to praise the Lord, but can walk the mall for four hours without sitting down. I am amazed at the people who will plunk down more than a hundred dollars for a pair of jeans, and then think they are doing something wonderful if they put a five dollar bill in the offering plate. I am amazed at the people who can

Your increase is dependent in part upon the degree to which you release your gifts to excellence.

spend hours and hours watching television, but can't seem to find an hour to pray.

God wants our best! He is worthy of our highest praise, our best gift, and our most excellent offerings.

How dare we approach Him with a casual attitude. How dare we approach Him with our second-rate effort and our second-rate giving. He is the Lord of Lords, the King of Kings, the Almighty God, the Sovereign of the Universe!

What audacity we have when we give God inferior time, energy, effort, and resources and then *expect* His best in return!

Get the Bigger Picture

Don't limit yourself when it comes to the fullness God has for you. Don't limit yourself when it comes to your giving. Your giving is directly linked to your receiving.

For a person to experience genuine increase, all of these principles related to giving need to be heeded:

- You are called to give your entire self to God.

- Your harvest from God will be far more than economic—trust God to meet *all* your needs.

- Your giving and receiving is primarily to be in the church where God has planted you.

- Your *tithe* obligates God to pour out His blessings.

- You are to give prayerfully and with faith.

- You must always give God your *best*.

Chapter 8

The Promise of
Debt-Free Living

A man recently asked if he could come to me for credit counseling. I told him to bring every credit card and every time-payment coupon book he had. When he arrived, he dumped the contents of a brown envelope onto my desk. There must have been at least twenty credit cards and time-payment books! He was borrowing from some cards to pay the minimum payments on other cards. The result was spiraling interest charges and an ever-growing mound of debt.

We worked out a plan for this man to tackle his debt, but I knew as he left my office that he faced a long and difficult road. It can take only moments for a person to get into debt—it sometimes can take years to climb out of it.

In today's society, borrowing is a given—an accepted way of life. People borrow money not only for houses and cars, but for vacations, clothing, luxury items, and just about everything else. In fact, at the dawn of the new millennium, Americans had close to $780 billion in outstanding consumer credit.

What is God's perspective on borrowing and debt? In every case where borrowing is discussed in the Bible, it is either discouraged or negatively addressed.

You may be asking, "What exactly is considered a debt?" Debt is when you cannot repay what you have promised. As long as you meet the payments you have agreed to make, you are not in debt. When you fail to make those payments, you are in debt. Debt results, very simply, when we spend more than we have, or when we put ourselves into a position of *needing* to borrow money or possessions.

Does this mean that a Christian should never use a credit card or purchase a house or car on time? No. At times borrowing is necessary. A person should never borrow, however, beyond his means to comfortably repay the debt. And above all, a person should never borrow at the expense of giving to God what God commands: the tithe and offerings. To give interest charges to a secular bank and fail to give to God what is commanded in His Word is an error that can greatly damage one's position before the Lord and that can greatly diminish the *increase* that God desires to give!

Debt Is Bondage

Why is debt considered to be so negative? Proverbs 22:7 gives us the answer: "The borrower is servant to the lender." When you borrow, you are putting yourself under the authority of the person or company from which you have borrowed. God wants His people to be solely under *His* authority—at all times and in all areas of life.

Debt is a bondage and God does not want His people to be in bondage. Indebtedness is a silent killer—of marriages, of attitude, of integrity, of hope. It can seriously damage a person's relationship with God.

God said to His people, "When the Lord your God blesses you as He promised you, then you shall lend to many nations, but you shall not borrow; and you shall rule over many nations, but they shall not rule over you." (Deut. 15:6; see also Deut. 28:12)

In the Old Testament, one of the curses associated with disobedience is this: "The transient (stranger) among you shall mount up higher and higher above you, and you shall come down lower and lower. He shall lend to you, but you shall not lend to him; he shall be the head, and you shall be the tail." (Deut. 28:43–44)

What should a person do if he is in debt? Seek every possible way to get out of debt! There is only one absolute when it comes to paying debt: If you borrow, you must pay back what you borrow. (See the story about a borrowed ax head in II Kings 6:1–7.) If you have borrowed something which you cannot presently repay, ask God to help you find a way to restore what you have borrowed. Ask Him to help you get out of debt and stay out of debt.

Trying to move into increase with a heavy load of debt is like trying to run a fifty-yard dash with your ankles shackled. Debt is the very antithesis of increase—the two cannot co-exist.

Wisdom in Handling Money

For many people, the problem of debt is rooted in a lack of understanding how to handle money. If you do not understand the basic economic principles related to money, bank accounts, credit accounts, and so forth, seek information. Free courses are available through many organizations, including many churches.

I have read a number of stories through the years about people who have become overnight millionaires by winning state lotteries. In the majority of these instances, the people who have won large sums of money have found themselves broke or struggling financially within a few years. Why? Because they were not prepared to handle the wealth that came their way. They were especially prone to fraud and mismanagement of their funds.

In many cases, the patterns of spending they manifested when they were "poor" continued on after they became "rich." These very patterns that had kept them poor in the first place caused them to become poor again. For example, they spent what they received rather than saving or investing some of the money, they overextended their credit, they invested in shady schemes, or they allowed others to influence their spending in ways that brought them little or no return. They lived out the old axiom, "A fool and his money are soon parted."

Ask God to impart to you *His* wisdom for dealing with money. There's much in the Bible on this subject. Use a concordance to get to the heart of the matter. Look up such topics as riches, money, lend, borrow, possessions, the rich, the poor, debt, and usury (interest).

Check Your Attitude about Money

For some, a lack of wisdom in handling money is not a matter of information as much as it is a matter of attitude. Many people have very poor self-esteem, and they believe that "spending" and "owning" certain possessions is a way of increasing their value in society or their social status. Others grew up with a prevailing mind-set, "We're poor." This atmosphere of poverty shackles them from moving into increase.

I grew up in a family that didn't have much money and had very few possessions, but I never thought we were lacking. We always had a roof over our heads, clothes on our backs, food in our stomachs, and love in our hearts. You can't be poor if you are rich in the love of the Lord and the love of family members!

I have met people who had plenty of money, but they *thought* they were poor. They were pre-occupied with how little they had and how tenuously they held what they had.

I have met people who had very little money, and they also thought they were poor. They were pre-occupied with how little they had and the hopelessness of the future stretched before them.

Poverty has very little to do with money. It has to do with what you believe, what you hope, how you think and dream, and in whom you place your trust. If you put your faith in

---

Poverty has very little to do with money. It has to do with what you believe, what you hope, how you think and dream, and in whom you place your trust.

---

yourself...you are trusting in a limited, finite, error-filled source. You can't help but think you are impoverished because you are trusting in a "poor" source! If you put your trust in the infinite God—and I mean really *trust* God—you can't think of yourself as poor. You are connected to the Source of all riches. You are linked by covenant to a perfect God with everything you need and desire at His disposal!

Breaking the Curse of Generational Poverty

Have you given your children a biblical inheritance? Have you taught them the Word and showed them by your example that the Word applies to every circumstance and situation of life, including finances?

In many ways, my mother determined my spiritual prosperity and destiny even before I was born. She had a covenant with God. I had a right to choose or not choose that destiny, but my mother had determined it.

Now my mother was not a theologian. I don't think she had ever read a book about the covenant. She knew the Word of God, however, to the point that she knew she could trust God with her children. She trusted God to help her live a godly life and to pass on a biblical inheritance to her children. She trusted God to help her teach me and my siblings the Bible and to show us by her example that we needed to be in church every Sunday to hear the Word of God preached and taught. She built into us a deep knowing that God was our Source of all protection, provision, and power.

Have you entrusted your children to God? Have you built a foundation for them on which they can build their faith, overcome fear, come to trust God as their Shield, and worship God alone—bowing down to no company, no institution, no governmental agencies, and no other person as the source of their total supply in life?

What you do regarding the Lord will impact your children, your grandchildren, your great-grandchildren, and your great-great grandchildren! The Word of God says:

> You shall not make yourself any graven image
> [to worship it] or any likeness of anything that is
> in the heavens above, or that is in the earth beneath,
> or that is in the water under the earth;
> You shall not bow down yourself to them or
> serve them; for I the Lord your God am a jealous
> God, visiting the iniquity of the fathers upon the
> children to the third and fourth generation of those
> who hate Me,
> But showing mercy and steadfast love to a
> thousand generations of those who love Me and
> keep My commandments. (Exod. 20:4–6)

Who suffers if a man becomes a drug lord or a murderer? Who suffers if a woman becomes a prostitute?

It is not only the person who sins who is affected. The children are also impacted in dramatic ways. The consequences have nothing to do with the sin of the child or of God's judgment on the child—rather, the consequences are the result of the parent's sin.

If there is a pattern of sin regarding money, or for that matter a pattern of sin regarding any area of life, ask the Lord to deliver you from that generational sin. Ask other Bible-believing Christians to pray with you about this matter. And then ask the Lord to show you how to "reverse the curse." Ask God to impart to you wisdom so that you might not repeat the patterns of old.

You may have grown up in a family that habitually overspends and has no concept of how to manage money wisely. You may have grown up in a family that devalues work. A relative in your past may have been involved in thievery or embezzlement. Someone in your past may have been involved in gain through unlawful means. Someone in your family tree may have been extremely greedy or may have used money as bribes to manipulate the behavior of others. There are numerous patterns of behavior related to money, possessions, prosperity, and blessings that may have been established in the generations before you that were contrary to God's Word and, therefore, were sinful.

The sin of your ancestors has established a pattern, a way of thinking and believing, a spiritual "hold" on your life.

I don't know the specific bondage that may have been placed on your family in the past. You may not know the behavior that resulted in a curse of poverty on you or your family. What I do know is that you can break that curse in the name of Jesus.

Teach Your Child To Make God the Source of Their "Salary." In Genesis 15:1 we read these encouraging words: "After these things, the word of the Lord came to Abram in a vision, saying, Fear not, Abram, I am your Shield, your abundant compensation, and your reward shall be exceedingly great."

What is the context for this great statement of Abram's trust in God?

Abram had just returned from the defeat of Chedorlaomer and the kings who were with him in order to free Lot, his nephew, who had been taken captive. Chedorlaomer had also taken all the wealth of Sodom and Gomorrah, which Abram also recovered. After Abram returned, the king of Sodom said to him, "Give me the persons and keep the goods for yourself." Abram had responded, "I have lifted up my hand and sworn to the Lord, God Most High, the Possessor and Maker of heaven and earth, That I would not take a thread or a shoelace or anything that is yours, lest you should say, I have made Abram rich. [Take all] except only what my young men have eaten and the share of the men [allies] who went with me—let them take their portion." (See Gen. 14.)

God honored the trust of Abram, again promising him a child. Then God entered into a blood-covenant relationship with Abram that night, and at that time God said to him, "Know positively that your descendants will be strangers dwelling as temporary residents in a land that is not theirs [Egypt], and they will be slaves there and will be afflicted and oppressed for 400 years. But I will bring judgment on that nation whom they will serve, and afterward they will come out with great possessions. And in the fourth generation they [your descendants] shall come back here [to Canaan] again, for the iniquity of the Amorites is not yet full and complete." (Gen. 15:13–14, 16)

God revealed to Abram that there would be rough times ahead for his descendants.

God revealed to Abram that there would be rough times ahead for his descendants. They would be afflicted and oppressed, and not just for a brief moment. They would live in slavery for four hundred years! But...what an important word that is! BUT... God then said the descendants of Abram would come out of that bondage with great possessions, and they would return to Canaan and occupy it fully.

Later God affirmed this promise to Abram, saying, "I will give to you and to your posterity after you the land in which you are a stranger [going from place to place], all the land of Canaan, for an everlasting possession; and I will be their God." (Gen. 17:8)

Abram trusted in God alone to be his Source—his salary-giver, his benefactor, his supplier. Abram's faithfulness in keeping his vow to God in the defeat of Chedorlaomer resulted in tremendous reward for himself *and for his children.* And Abram built that trust into his son Isaac, and he into his son Jacob, and he into his son Joseph. The descendants of Abram trusted God to provide for them, even when they were forced into slavery.

Teach your children to trust God in every area of their lives, including their finances. Here are some very practical ways in which you can break the cycle of generational poverty and establish a cycle of generational prosperity:

• Give your tithe and offerings to the Lord. Put yourself and your family into a position to receive God's provision. Teach your children to give. Show them by your example that you are trusting God to pour out the riches of heaven upon you and all in your family. Be faithful in your giving.

• When you hear news about negative economic trends, including down-turns, recessions, depressions, and any other type of economic hardship, assure your children that you are trusting God to provide for you. Rather than convey fear over an uncertain economic future, build faith in your children regarding God's power to provide.

• Encourage your children to memorize God's promises related to provision. Also encourage your children to memorize various verses in Proverbs that relate to the wise use of money and possessions.

• Read to your children true-life stories about God's provision—both stories from the Bible and modern-day stories in which God has been faithful to meet the needs of His people. Give your children an arsenal of examples to bolster their faith.

• Let your children hear you pray for provision, asking God to meet *all* of your needs. Let them hear faith in your voice as you pray!

God desires for His people to be on the top, not the bottom—to be the head, not the tail. He wants His people to be debt-free. Then, and only then, can they move fully into the *abundance* of increase He desires to give them.

Chapter 9

The Promise of
God's Timing in Increase

An economist was reading his Bible one day and he came across this verse, "With the Lord one day is as a thousand years, and a thousand years as one day" (2 Peter 3:8 NKJV). He prayed to the Lord, "Is this really true, Lord? Is a thousand years to me really like only one day to You? Does that mean an entire year to me is like a fraction of a second to You?"

The Lord spoke back to his heart, "Yes, that's correct."

The economist then projected, "Well, if a thousand years is like a day, then is a million dollars to me like only a penny to You?"

The Lord said, "Yes, that's correct also."

The economist said, "Well, Lord, then surely it isn't too much for me to ask You to give me a penny or two?"

The Lord replied, "All right. Come back in a few minutes and I'll have it ready for you."

God is never going to be rushed when it comes to the timing of your increase.

God is never going to be rushed when it comes to the timing of your increase. He is never going to take short-cuts. He is concerned with every *detail* of your life and mine. He is going to "do it right" in our lives. His will manifested *through* you is going to impact His entire Kingdom, and He is one hundred percent committed to accomplishing the fullness of His purposes for His Kingdom on this earth.

People sometimes ask me, "Tony, why would God be so concerned about all the details of my life?" Because you are part of God's bigger picture. The details of your life are part of the details of His total plan for this world and for the development of His Kingdom. God is not concerned about you alone, but about every person whose life is impacted, touched, or influenced by you, not only now, but in days and weeks and years to come.

When God makes a promise, He does not look at His wristwatch. He does not link a promise to a particular time frame, after which His promise is null and void. When God said to the children of Israel, "I am going to take you to the land of promise," He did not tell them it would happen in six weeks, six months, or six years. The time could have been much shorter than the forty years that it turned out to be had the Israelites trusted God and entered directly into Canaan after they first spied out the land. In fact, they could have entered into the land in less than two months.

The time frame put on the fulfillment of the promise was not given by God—rather, the assurance that the promise would be fulfilled.

Disobedience Can Delay Increase. An important principle about God's timing is this: We cannot "rush" God's perfecting work in us, but we *can* hinder or delay God's perfecting work by refusing to cooperate with Him. When we rebel against God, disobey His commands to us, or choose our own way over His, we can avert or detour God's plan for us. He will still make a way for us to get back on the main highway of His purposes for us...but our traveling time will be increased and the way will often be more difficult.

Cooperation with God keeps us on God's fast-track plan for His perfecting work, but we cannot "skip steps" or "take short-cuts" to experience His work in us and through us.

---

*God will meet your needs when the
needs need to be met. He will supply
your needs on a daily basis.*

Faith to Believe for "When." Just as our faith is required in believing "what" God desires to accomplish in our lives, so faith is required to believe "when" God will fulfill His promise. Most of us would like multiplication to occur in our lives overnight. We want instant everything in our world today—from instant foods to instant service to instant cures to instant profits. It takes faith to say, "I know God is going to act in the fullness of time— in the exact instance, the precise time period, the right moment."

You may think that God is overdue in bringing about your increase. Let me assure you that God is never late...and He is never early. He always acts and provides in exactly the right time to accomplish what He desires.

A number of Christians seem to think they don't need to discern matters of timing. They receive a promise from God and they forge headlong into the process they think is necessary for receiving that promise, never stopping to ask God, "When should I act? What is Your timetable?" When we fail to ask God about matters of timing and trust God to act in the fullness of time, we find ourselves making hasty statements that bring us embarrassment or cause us to apologize later. We find ourselves making unwise choices and decisions any time we move ahead of God.

Daily Needs, Daily Provision. Jesus taught His disciples to pray, "Give us this day our daily bread." (Matt. 6:11)

God will meet your needs *when* the needs need to be met. He will supply your needs on a daily basis.

When I took my son to enroll in college, I wrote a check for eight hundred dollars for his tuition...and then I hurried home to figure out a way to cover the rest of that year's expenses, which totaled about four thousand dollars. A second payment of two thousand dollars was due just a few weeks after that initial payment.

When I arrived home, a businessman called me and invited me to get coffee with him. We engaged in small talk at a coffee shop quite a ways across town. On the way back, he asked if it would be all right with me if he stopped by his office for a few minutes. He left the car running while he went into his office building and then he drove me back to my car. When we arrived there, he handed me an envelope with a check in it. It was for four thousand dollars. I said, "The church can sure use this!"

> *We must never lose sight of the fact that God exists outside of time—He is not bound by our twenty-four-hour days.*

He replied, "It isn't for the church. It's made out to you and it's for *you*. I just received a check for this amount from an insurance settlement and I asked the Lord what He wanted me to do with the money. He told me to give it to you to help you meet some special need in your life."

I said, "I can't accept this."

He said, "Are you going to deny my obedience in doing what the Lord told me to do?"

I accepted the check. And I wept all the way home.

No Ultimatums. For many of us, things don't seem to happen fast enough. Answers to our prayers don't come quickly enough. Especially if we have a "word from the Lord" or are involved in ministry, we seem to think that things should be happening faster to bring us the fulfillment of the promises we believe God has made to us.

We err greatly, however, when we try to give God an ultimatum regarding our increase, saying perhaps, "I want You to do this for me by this time next week" or "within the next ninety days." God is not bound by any ultimatums you may issue.

He will perform His plans and purposes for your life according to *His* timetable and *His* methods and always for *His* glory.

We must never lose sight of the fact that God exists outside of time—He is not bound by our twenty-four-hour days. He does not operate according to the earth's clock when it comes to the execution of His will. His plans and purposes are unfolding according to His schedule, which accommodates eternity.

Our role while we wait for the fulfillment of God's will in our lives is, very simply, to *trust God*.

What Is Our Position
as We Wait on the Lord?

I readily admit to you that I have struggled at times with patience. When I see something good that is from God, I want it in my life and in the life of those I love...and I want it sooner than later. I have often prayed the famous prayer, "Lord, give me patience, but please hurry up. I need it NOW."

What I have recognized from my own experience and as I have watched countless others "wait" for God's increase in their lives is this simple truth: God gives every person repeated opportunities as they wait on Him to demonstrate their humility before Him, their trust in Him, and their obedience to His Word.

These four things are what we are called to "do" as we wait.

1. Remain Humble. During our waiting period we must remain humble before God. We must acknowledge that *He* is doing a work in us and that all timing is subject to His purposes. We must declare repeatedly to our own minds and hearts that Jesus Christ is the author and finisher of our faith. (See Heb. 12:2.) We must accept that He is continuing to do the good work that He has started in us. As the apostle Paul wrote, we must be "confident of this very thing, that He who has begun a good work in you will complete it until the day of Jesus Christ." (Phil. 1:6 NKJV)

We must own up to our mistakes and ask the Lord to help us turn away from sin and toward righteousness at every opportunity.

We must ask God to strengthen our weaknesses...to heal our wounds...and to help us withstand all temptation.

The Bible admonishes us, "Don't overlook the obvious here, friends....God isn't late with his promise as some measure lateness. He is restraining himself on account of you, holding back the End because he doesn't want anyone lost. He's giving everyone space and time to change" (II Pet. 3:8–9 Message Bible)

God desires each of us to grow and to change. That's the only way we get from the place we are today—which is a place of imperfection—to the place God desires for us to be, which is a place of perfection and total conformity to Christ Jesus. (See Rom. 8:28–30.)

Ask the Lord today what *He* desires you to change in your life. Ask Him what *He* desires you to do. The position of humility calls us to bow before the Lord and pray as Jesus prayed, "Not My will, but Yours be done." (Luke 22:42)

2. Trust God in All Things. In *Sabbatical Journeys*, Henri Nouwen wrote about meeting a troupe of trapeze artists known as "The Flying Rudellas." The Rudellas told Nouwen about the very special relationship that develops between a "flyer" and a "catcher" in a trapeze act. The flyer is the person who lets go of his swing and does a stunt in the air, perhaps two or three somersaults. The catcher is the person who then reaches out and takes hold of the flyer and helps him get to the platform at the opposite side of the performance area. The flyer does not grab hold of the catcher—rather, the catcher is responsible for reaching out and grabbing hold of the flyer.

Nouwen wrote, "When the flyer is swinging high above the audience on the trapeze, the moment comes when he must let go. He arcs out into the air and his job is to remain as still as possible and wait for the strong hands of the catcher to pluck him out of the air. The flyer must never reach for the catcher. The catcher must take hold of the flyer."

What an amazing example of trust! The Lord is our catcher. He asks us to trust Him completely, regardless of our circumstances or the risky nature of His call to us. Do you ever feel that the Lord has asked you to go out on a limb for Him, to take a risk of your faith, or to say or do something you wouldn't normally have thought to say or do? It is your job to do what the Lord asks and then trust Him to catch you and guide you safely to your destination point.

Trust does not develop overnight, of course. There's no such thing as instant trust. Trust develops the more we spend time with a person and put a relationship to the test in many circumstances and under many conditions.

This is especially true for flyers and catchers. A flyer and a catcher spend a great deal of time together outside the circus tent. They get to know each other so well that they can almost complete each other's sentences and read each other's mind. They are sensitive to every nuance of timing and to every reaction and instinct of the other person. Only then can they safely perform their act.

Our trust in God develops in a like manner. We must spend time with the Lord, listening to what the Lord speaks to our heart. We must become so sensitive to God's desires that we instinctively move toward them. We must feel what God feels, see the world as God sees the world, and reach out to touch the world as Jesus touched the world. We truly are called not only to ask the question, "What would Jesus do?" but to know the ANSWER to that question and then DO what Jesus would do. Our trust in the Lord is put to the test daily.

We truly are called not only to ask the question, "What would Jesus do?" but to know the ANSWER to that question and then DO what Jesus would do.

3. Obey All of the Lord's Directives. In our society, there is a strong correlation between status and waiting for instructions. Those who are lower in status "wait" for a directive from those who have higher status or authority. A servant waits on his master to tell him what to do. An employee waits on his supervisor to give him his daily work orders. A chauffeur or taxi driver waits on the person he is driving to tell him where to drive. As believers...we are to wait on the Lord for our daily directives.

Some of those directives are simply to "do" the larger directives He has given us in His Word—the Ten Commandments and the many admonitions that are linked to the two great commandments: to love God and to love others as ourselves. Some of the Lord's directives to us are very specific and timebound—they are our working directives for any given hour, any given day.

Our role when faced with any of the Lord's commandments, statutes, directives, or admonitions is not to question them, seek to alter them, or dismiss them. Rather, we are to *do* them with our whole heart, mind, and soul. We are called—yes, commanded—to obey God with a quick and willing heart.

The hope of God's promises leads us to pursue God's will and commandments with our whole heart, without wavering or stopping. We are involved in a process that leads us into increased faith and spiritual authority.

I usually find that the quicker I set my attitude and heart to obey God, the sooner the Lord tells me what to do. Is it any mystery that God would speak more readily to the person with an open, willing, and obedient heart than to a person with a closed, unwilling, and rebellious heart?

Hebrews 10:36 tells us, "For you have need of endurance, so that after you have done the will of God, you may receive the promise." *After you have done the will of God.* Keeping God's commandments and obeying God—including accepting Jesus Christ as our Savior in obedience to God—is the supreme will of God for us.

Don't fling away your fire, energy, and zeal because the Lord hasn't answered your petition as soon as you had desired or requested. As the apostle Paul wrote to the Thessalonians: "Do not become weary or lose heart in doing right [but continue in well-doing without weakening]." (II Thess. 3:13)

Put your energy and zeal into doing what the Lord has put before you to do, clinging to God's promise and continuing to believe for it. The wellspring for our hope lies in God's giving the promise, not in our soon receiving the promise.

4. Keep Your Eyes on the Promise. I have heard people say, "How can you be so optimistic right now when *nothing* is happening?" The only way I can be optimistic is if I truly am clinging to a promise from God.

Waiting is not a time when we sit back and see what will happen. We are to wait with *expectation.* We are to keep our eyes on the promise that God has made to us in His Word, *fully expecting* God to be true to His Word and to do in us that which He has said He *will* do!

The Greek language in which the Bible was written has a number of meanings for the word "wait"—in various places in the New Testament, the word means to:

• look forward to and await (I Thess. 1:10)

• wait with patience and composure (Rom. 8:23–25)

• look forward to something with open anticipation, as if you would welcome a person into your presence

• receive something openly

• look for, with expectation

To wait patiently is to wait with eagerness and to be increasingly open to receive something.

Now, how does this relate to faith? Faith has been defined as the ability to see by the Spirit and in the Spirit those things that

---

Waiting is not a time when we sit back and see what will happen. We are to wait with expectation.

God desires to bring into our lives. Faith is seeing with inner eyes those things which are surely going to come to us and be worked in us because of God's promises to us.

With our faith we see *what* God intends to do for our eternal good. What is it that God has said in His Word He will do for you? When you encounter God's promises, your faith is ignited to say, "That promise is for *me*. God is going to do that for *me*. God is going to do that in *me*. God is going to do that through *me*." Faith is the substance of things we cannot yet see. In other words, it is seeing those things that are not accomplished at the present as if they are accomplished. Faith gives us a certainty that God is at work in our lives in a very personal, dynamic, and *certain* way.

Waiting is the hardest work of hope.

With our hope, we *trust* that God is at work in us even now to accomplish what He intends to do. Hope is an abiding and confident expectation that His good plan for us is being accomplished in us.

Lewis Snedes has said, "Waiting is our destiny. As creatures who cannot by themselves bring about what they hope for, we wait in the darkness for a flame we cannot light, we wait in fear for a happy ending we cannot write, we wait for a 'not yet' that feels like a 'not ever.'"

Waiting is the hardest work of hope.

When we allow hope to die out, we begin to settle for second-best in our lives rather than God's *very best*.

Our hope must be inextinguishable. We are the ones who make that choice to keep hope alive and burning in us or a choice to say, "I no longer have hope in that area or circumstance of my life." Don't let any storm of life put out the flame of hope in your heart!

Chapter 10

The Increase We Can Experience As We "Wait"

How do you feel about waiting?

I have never heard a person say, "I *love* to wait. I *love* to sit in waiting rooms and stand in long lines."

Far more important than your feelings about waiting is your understanding about how God uses the waiting process to make us what He wants us to be.

God desires that we *become* something, and it is in the waiting time that He molds us and fashions us and makes us into the people He desires us to be.

As I watched the last Summer Olympic Games, I saw a cyclist take a terrible fall. As she picked up her damaged cycle and got back on it, obviously in pain, the announcer commented, "For four years she has lived for this moment." For four years, this woman had trained for a few minutes of competition—she had watched her diet, strengthened her muscles, and practiced her cycling. For four years, she "waited" for the Olympic competition to arrive, but her waiting was not idle. It was purposeful, diligent, focused, and filled with activities to *prepare* her for the moment of competition and victory.

What did her future hold? Four more years of the same...four more years of waiting and preparing and continuing to increase her strength, endurance, ability, and competitive edge.

Was all this "waiting" time a waste because she lost? No. She was a stronger, more patient, more focused, more motivated, more fit, more disciplined, and more persevering person—*not because she won the race, but because she had used her waiting period to full advantage.* The most important values to be gained from her athletic training were developing in her life *during the waiting period.* They didn't come as a result of her victory in one race, rather in her *preparing* for that goal day in and day out.

As believers in Christ Jesus, we are called to *drive* toward the prize of the promise God has for us. We are to train diligently for the day in which God will give the victory!

Preparing Ourselves for What God Has Prepared

In every area of my life in which God seems to have me "on hold," He is doing something *in* me to perfect me to take the next step He has for me. He is perfecting me in order to use me in the way He has already planned to use me.

The apostle Paul wrote to the Romans: "For those whom He foreknew [of whom He was aware and loved beforehand], He also destined from the beginning [foreordaining them] to be molded into the image of His Son [and share inwardly His likeness], that He might become the firstborn among many brethren." (Rom. 8:29)

The prosperity message is often aimed at "comfort"—we desire certain blessings in order to be more comfortable. The Bible message of whole-life increase is all about "conformation"—God is in the process of making and molding us into the image of His Son so that we "share inwardly His likeness."

What God does in us while we wait is as important as that thing for which we are waiting.

The apostle Paul declared to the Romans:

> [Let us also be full of joy now!] let us exult
> and triumph in our troubles and rejoice in our
> sufferings, knowing that pressure and affliction and

hardship produce patient and unswerving endurance.

And endurance (fortitude) develops maturity of character (approved faith and tried integrity). And character [of this sort] produces [the habit of] joyful and confident hope of eternal salvation. (Rom. 5:3–4)

Look at the things Paul says are accomplished in us while we wait: perseverance or "unswerving endurance;" a real maturity of character, an "approved faith," and a tried-and-true integrity; a character that "produces joyful and confident hope." This work that is done *in* us while we wait is *eternal work*. It is a work that molds and makes us into the person God desires us to be.

What happens to us as we wait? We change on the inside and are renewed in the spirit. This work that happens on the *inside* of us is just as important as any outward manifestation. Isaiah 40:31 declares:

But those who wait for the Lord [who expect, look for, and hope in Him] shall change and renew their strength and power; they shall lift their wings and mount up [close to God] as eagles [mount up to the sun]; they shall run and not be weary, they shall walk and not faint or become tired.

As we wait on God's timing—using that waiting period to full advantage as we hone our gifts, increase our praise to the Lord, and employ our gifts in obedient service to the Lord at all stages of development—we increase in *strength and power*. We grow in our ability to persevere and endure.

Waiting Increases Us on the Inside

In the Message Bible, Romans 8:22–25 reads:

All around us we observe a pregnant creation. The difficult times of pain throughout the world are simply birth pangs. But it's not only around us; it's *within* us. The Spirit of God is arousing us within. We're also feeling the birth pangs. These sterile and barren bodies of ours are yearning for full deliverance. That is why waiting does not diminish us, any more than waiting diminishes a pregnant mother. We are enlarged in the waiting. We, of course, don't see what is enlarging us. But the longer we wait, the larger we become, and the more joyful our expectancy.

A pregnant woman is not *decreased* in her waiting...she is *increased*. So, too, with us as we wait for God's full increase to be perfected in us, through us, and around us.

We must come to the point where we not only accept, but appreciate the waiting process.

There are two things waiting is *NOT* intended to be.

First, waiting is NOT passive. It is not an irresponsible shirking of responsibility, saying, "Well, I'm just going to wait to see what God does. If He wants something done, He'll do it and I'm going to wait on the sidelines and see what happens." Waiting can sometimes become an excuse for not taking responsibility or appropriate action. It can be a form of living in denial.

Waiting is *active* anticipation. It is enduring in what we know to do *until* God's answer is manifested. It is standing up to the trials of life and actively seeking to overcome life's problems with a firm expectation that God is at work and His answers will be revealed.

Waiting is active anticipation. It is enduring in what we know to do until God's answer is manifested.

While we wait, we do what God has put in our path to do.

A farmer *waits* for the harvest from the seed he plants in the spring. Does that mean that he sits down at the edge of the field and watches to see what will sprout and produce?

No! He tends the field—he weeds, waters, cultivates the soil, applies the fertilizer, and deals with the insects that might destroy his crop. He *works*...but nevertheless, he *waits*. He is filled with expectation that the seed *will* produce in the fullness of time and that a harvest is on the way.

At the heart of patience must be obedient service. We must *do* what the Lord calls us to do. It is in obedient service that our gifts are refined and our hearts are softened.

The psalmist declares,

> The eyes of all wait for You [looking, watching, and expecting] and You give them their food in due season. You open Your hand and satisfy every living thing with favor.
>
> The Lord is [rigidly] righteous in all His ways and gracious and merciful in all His works.
>
> The Lord is near to all who call upon Him, to all who call upon Him sincerely and in truth.
>
> He will fulfill the desires of those who reverently and worshipfully fear Him; He also will hear their cry and will save them. (Ps. 145:15–19)

In God's timing, He gives us sustenance and "satisfies" our every heart's desire with "favor." Does this mean that God is distant from us during the waiting period? No! He is near to all who call upon Him. He hears our heart's cries. He receives our worship. He delights in our praise. Our stance as we wait is a stance of genuine service to the Lord—to grow in our fellowship with the Lord, to enter into a daily communion with the Lord, to grow increasingly dependent upon the Lord for direction and guidance, and to place more and more of our trust in Him to be our Provider, Protector, Savior, and Lord.

To wait upon the Lord means to give God the reigns of our life. We must learn to get out of the "control" business when it comes to determining *what* we will be and *when* our time of increase will arrive. God determines our gifts. He has built them into us from our birth. In like manner, it is God who determines when our times of increase and harvest will come.

Second, waiting is NOT undisciplined. Waiting is focused. While we wait, we must fix our will and mind upon the Lord—waiting is a time of disciplined clinging to God. We must maintain our devotion to God. We must focus on the things of His Kingdom. We must be ready at any moment to act in whatever way God may direct us to act—to say what He desires us to say in any conversation, to go where He tells us to go, and to do what He tells us to do.

God is always in the process of preparing us for the work He has prepared for us.

We are to wait with an intentional expectation that at any moment God might give us a directive that will position us to take the next step He has for us. We are to be alert for every opportunity that God sends our way.

Most of God's directives to us during the waiting season will be directives to serve others.

Every act of service to others is an act of "waiting" on the Lord—of trusting Him to guide you to those who need your gift, relying on Him to help you give your best in everything you do, and expecting Him to use your gifts for the enlargement of His Kingdom and the refinement and enlargement of your own life.

God is always in the process of preparing us for the work He has prepared for us. We never outgrow that process. We use our gifts and as we use our gifts, we grow in our gifts. We grow in our ability to hear God's voice in our spirit. We grow in our desire to be of use to Him. As our gifts grow and we become more sensitive to God's leading, we find new opportunities to use our gifts. As we use our enlarged gifts, our gifts grow even larger! The more we act on the impulses of the Holy Spirit in our hearts, the more God seems to speak to us and the more clearly we discern His will for us. Our waiting on the Lord is a process of continually growing both inwardly and outwardly.

When We Become Weary of Waiting

The apostle Paul also wrote to the Romans:

> "The moment we get tired in the waiting, God's Spirit is right alongside helping us along. If we don't know how or what to pray, it doesn't matter. He does our praying in and for us, making prayer out of our wordless sighs, our aching groans. He knows us far better than we know ourselves, knows our pregnant condition, and keeps us present before God. That's why we can be so sure that every detail in our lives of love for God is worked into something good." (Rom. 8:26–28 Message Bible)

When we get tired in our waiting, God is there to help us.

God is the One who picks the times and seasons of our lives. He knows when we are ready to have a dream planted into our lives. He knows when we need to have that dream cultivated or watered or pruned. He knows when the time is right for us to experience a harvest.

The Bible tells us that in the fullness of time God sent His Son Jesus to this earth. There was an exact time of "fullness"— of readiness, completeness, and perfection for Jesus to be born. The Bible says that in due season God's will is perfected. Galatians 6:9 says it plainly, "Let us not lose heart and grow weary and faint in acting nobly and doing right, for in due time and at the appointed season we shall reap, if we do not loosen and relax our courage and faint."

Psalm 1:3 also speaks of God's perfecting work in the life of the godly person: "He shall be like a tree firmly planted [and tended] by the streams of water, ready to bring forth its fruit in its season; its leaf also shall not fade or wither; and everything he does shall prosper [and come to maturity]."

One type of palm tree requires three years for the seed to sprout through the surface of the earth. The seed produces roots during the first three years, reaching down toward the water table underlying the arid soil. The roots literally "tap into" a source of life-giving nutrients and refreshment. Only after the roots are established does this particular species of palm put up a sprout into the desert air.

The growing process then continues for twenty years before the palm produces its sweetest fruit and its most abundant harvest. And at what time of year does this fruit appear? At the driest and hottest part of the summer!

What a lesson in delayed gratification!

Our responsibility before the Lord is not to produce the harvest, rather to seek the Lord and establish a relationship with Him. He is the Source of our life. He is the Author of our purpose. He is the Creator of all things necessary for the fulfillment of His purpose for our life on the earth. The longer we live in total reliance upon Him, the sweeter and more productive our lives become. We are able to produce even in the toughest of times because we have diligently and consistently sought the Lord day in and day out—not just for a few weeks or months, but for years and even decades.

Waiting May Last a Lifetime or Longer

In Genesis mankind is called to await the promised seed that will redeem man from his sinful state.

In Revelation mankind is depicted as waiting for the "day of the Lord" when the Lord takes His chosen ones from the earth.

Throughout the Scriptures between Genesis and Revelation, we find numerous examples of people who are called to wait— some of them for a lifetime and some of them for even longer than a lifetime!

Abraham waited twenty-five years between the time God first promised him an heir until the birth of Isaac.

Moses spent forty years in Egypt and forty years in exile on the backside of the desert before he led the Israelites out of slavery.

The children of Israel wandered in the wilderness forty years before God led them across the Jordan River into Canaan. That meant that Joshua and Caleb waited forty years before they stepped into the position God had for them in the Promise Land.

Simeon and Anna were in the Temple year after year, serving the Lord, until the day finally came when they saw the baby Jesus and knew that the promised Messiah had arrived.

Jesus spent thirty years in preparation for three years of active ministry.

Don't become discouraged at the length of time you may experience between the time you receive the promise of God and the time you receive the fulfillment of that promise. God is at work all the time—enlarging you, working in you, and conforming you into the image of Christ Jesus so you will be *ready* for the enlarged place and enlarged path that God has for you!

Chapter 11

The Promise of Many Methods of Multiplication

For several years while both of my children were in college, the man who helped me with my taxes said to me, "I don't know how you do it. You should be in debt. You shouldn't be making ends meet financially."

I said, "God helps us." He said, "You don't make enough money to send these kids to college without debt, and yet somehow you do."

We never borrowed a dime for our children's educations and our children never received a grant. We were on the borderline—we made just enough in salary that our children did not qualify for government grants, yet we made too little to be able in the natural to pay the bills for all of their college expenses. God sovereignly sent special opportunities for us to earn extra income, or He sovereignly moved on people's hearts to help us with college expenses. The provision was always there, sometimes just in the nick of time.

When the time came for my daughter to marry, we experienced a similar miracle. I didn't have the money on deposit to give her the type of wedding she desired. The money came, however, from some of the least likely sources. It did not come because we planted a specific one-time offering. It came because we had spent twenty years planting ourselves into the lives of people and into a community.

We have discussed in previous chapters that faith is necessary to believe God for the "what" and the "when" of your increase. Faith is also required to trust God for "how." We must allow God to use His methods, not our methods.

The person who believes firmly that God is going to accomplish a specific work in his life and who is trusting God to work according to His eternal timetable, often fails at this point. It's all too human to say, "I know how this should be done." We are quick to tell God which methods to use, which protocols to follow, and which systems to employ.

The fact is, God knows precisely not only what He desires to do and when, but how He intends to accomplish His goals. God acts in ways that bring Him the greatest amount of glory, produce the greatest opportunities for a person to accept Jesus as their Savior, and yield the greatest harvest of blessing for the greatest number of people. God acts according to His ways and means, which the prophet Isaiah assures us are "higher" than our ways. Let me remind you of this passage from God's Word:

> For My thoughts are not your thoughts, neither are your ways My ways, says the Lord.
>
> For as the heavens are higher than the earth, so are My ways higher than your ways and My thoughts than your thoughts.
>
> For as the rain and snow come down from the heavens, and return not there again, but water the earth and make it bring forth and sprout, that it may give seed to the sower and bread to the eater,
>
> So shall My word be that goes forth out of My mouth: it shall not return to Me void [without producing any effect, useless], but it shall accomplish that which I please and purpose, and it shall prosper in the thing for which I sent it. (Isa. 55:8–11)

God is not limited to natural means. He operates in the supernatural.

God is not limited to humanly engineered systems, although He often uses people to accomplish His will.

God is not limited to specific agencies, bureaucratic channels, or political protocols. He is the Sovereign King. He makes up the rules by which He functions.

Never limit God when it comes to how He might work in your life. He is likely to move and act in the very way you least expect.

God's Advance Preparation

Before God ever calls you to do anything, He has already provided for your success in that calling.

In I Kings 17, we find the story of Elijah, who prophesied, "As the Lord, the God of Israel, lives, before Whom I stand, there shall not be dew or rain these years but according to My word." (I Kings 17:1)

This certainly wasn't an encouraging word to Ahab, the king. Elijah knew his life would be in danger. Furthermore, there was no assurance to him personally that the righteous of the Lord would be spared the famine that would surely result from such a severe lack of rainfall.

Then the Word of the Lord came to Elijah again, saying, "Go from here and turn east and hide yourself by the brook Cherith, east of the Jordan. You shall drink of the brook, and I have commanded the ravens to feed you there." (I Kings 17:3–4)

God provided protection and provision for Elijah. Note that all-important phrase, "I have commanded the ravens." God had already prepared the way for Elijah even before He placed His prophecy in Elijah's mouth. And the ravens brought Elijah bread and flesh in the morning and in the evening, and he drank water from the brook until the famine became so severe that the brook dried up.

When the brook was dry, the Lord again spoke to Elijah, "Arise, go to Zarephath, which belongs to Sidon, and dwell there.

Behold, I have commanded a widow there to provide for you." (I Kings 17:9) Again, we read "I have commanded"—this time, a widow. God again prepared the way for Elijah in advance.

If God calls you to a particular place, you can be assured that He has already prepared the way for you in advance of His call to you. God does not "wing it" as we human beings often do. He is purposeful. He has a plan that He is in the process of implementing, and that plan is complete. It has protection, provision, and blessings built into it for those who obey His call.

One Step at a Time

Elijah may have thought when God told him to go to a widow, Aha! A widow. Her husband must have left her well fixed in life if she is going to take care of me. If that's what he was anticipating, imagine his surprise when he showed up at her doorstep and found her gathering sticks and planning to prepare one last little cake of meal and oil for her son and herself. No inheritance. No servants. No palatial living conditions. No overflowing provision.

For her part, the widow had been commanded by God to feed the prophet. She may very well have been anticipating that he would show up with the provisions for her to cook! If that's what she was anticipating, imagine her surprise when he showed up empty-handed and then asked that she give to him her last little bit of oil and meal.

Don't try to second-guess God's methods. Don't try to read instant success into anything God commands you to do. There is always a process involved and that process invariably requires faith, wisdom, and effort.

What this prophet did have was a Word from the Lord: "For thus says the Lord, the God of Israel: The jar of meal shall not waste away or the bottle of oil fail until the day that the Lord sends rain on the earth." (I Kings 17:14) What the widow did have was a willingness to act in faith and to do as He asked. Both were willing to be one hundred percent obedient to the Lord.

And look what God did with their obedience. He multiplied the oil and meal just as He had promised and in the next three years of famine, they may have eaten more than a thousand meals from the provision of the Lord.

Their needs were met one day at a time. Every day the widow had to cook a "last meal." Every day she saw the bottom of the oil jar and the bottom of the meal jar. The total supply for years of food was not given—indeed, if it had been given it would have been subject to spoiling.

Your needs are met in the same way—daily. We must never lose sight of the fact that God deals with us on a day-by-day basis. The Lord told us to pray, "Give us this day our daily bread."

God provides for most of us a staircase from where we are—upward, onward, and forward—to the "top" He has envisioned for us.

(Matt. 6:11) God can, and He may, dump a fortune into your lap overnight, but in the vast majority of cases, God provides for us day by day. Our walk of faith is a daily walk. Our needs are met daily. The overall trend of our lives is increase. We must accept and work for slow and steady steps of increase.

Think for a moment of a high wall, perhaps twenty-five feet high. Nobody could take a giant step or a giant leap and end up at the top of that wall, not even with pole vaulting equipment. What a person can do is build a series of steps that leads up the side of that wall. To get to the top of that wall, then, requires that a person take one step at a time—something that any able-bodied person can do. In fact, the more shallow the steps—which means the more steps involved—the easier the climb is going to be.

God provides for most of us a staircase from where we are— upward, onward, and forward—to the "top" He has envisioned for us. He gives us the strength and energy to take one step at a time—but we must do the stepping. He does not transport us from the bottom to the top in an instant. He requires that we trust Him to move upward just a few inches at a time. Sometimes the steps are steep and more difficult to take; at other times they are shallow steps and easier to take. We face a daily task of taking one step at a time.

I encourage you today, get your eyes off the height of the wall and onto the next step upward!

God Accomplishes His Purposes

Regardless of the method God uses to supply your increase, you can be assured of two things:

- Man can slow down and detour God's plans, but neither man nor the devil can stop what God has purposed. God will accomplish His purposes. He will fulfill His promises to you as you trust Him with the what, when, and how of His provision.
- God always deals in terms of multiplication. The end result of increase is not a "little" bit added to your total life. God says to all men and women, from the first man and woman onward— "Be fruitful and multiply."

The word multiply in its various forms appears more than nine hundred times in the Bible. You will find it from cover to cover. The end of multiplication is "myriad," a term originating in the Greek language to refer to a number that is too vast to be calculated or counted.

Trust God today to accomplish His multiplication of your life. And to do it in His way.

Chapter 12

The Place of Your Increase

God has always had a place for His people. From Genesis to Revelation, we find this truth confirmed—God has a place for *you*.

Along with giving you gifts and talents and callings, God has assignments, locations, and "connections" expressly and uniquely for you. He has a *place* for you. In all ways, God has prepared and continues to prepare you to flourish in the place He has for you. It is a place that is glorious and intended to be marked by all that is pure, righteous, and true.

For Adam and Eve, that place was the Garden of Eden. God blessed Adam and Eve there and "God blessed them, and said to them, Be fruitful, multiply, and fill the earth, and subdue it [using all its vast resources in the service of God and man]; and have dominion over the fish of the sea, the birds of the air, and over every living creature that moves upon the earth." (Gen. 1:28)

The place God had for Adam and Eve was a place of great increase. It was a *good* place—everything in it was suitable, pleasant, and fully approved by God. *All* of it was given to Adam and Eve—every plant, every tree, every animal, every bird, and every creature that crept on the ground.

God had a place for Noah. The first place He had for him was an ark, a place of safety to ride out a time of massive destruction. The second place He had for him was a renewed earth. And it, too, was a place of increase. God said to Noah, "Be fruitful and multiply and fill the earth...be fruitful and multiply; bring forth abundantly on the earth and multiply on it." (Gen. 9:1, 7)

God had a place for Abram. He called to Abram in Haran and said, "Go for yourself [for your own advantage] away from your country, from your relatives and your father's house, to the land that I will show you. And I will make of you a great nation, and I will bless you [with abundant increase of favors] and make your name famous and distinguished, and you will be a blessing [dispensing good to others]." (Gen. 12:1–2)

God expanded on this promise in Genesis 17:6—"I will make you exceedingly fruitful and I will make nations of you, and kings will come from you." The blessing extended to Ishmael: "I will bless him and will make him fruitful and will multiply him exceedingly; He will be the father of twelve princes, and I will make him a great nation." (Gen. 17:20)

Throughout Scripture when God calls a person, He leads that person to a place of increase that benefits both the person involved, as well as others who are God's people. God leads people to places where His Kingdom is going to be established and increased.

God called Abraham to a *land* of increase.

He called Moses to a *land* of promise that would be overflowing with "milk and honey"—great Bible symbols of increase.

He called the prophet Jonah to a place called Ninevah to proclaim His message, with the intent that the Ninevites would repent and experience increase in their lives.

He sent Jesus, His only Son, to a place called earth to secure the salvation of mankind and increase His Kingdom.

He sent the apostle Paul to specific cities to proclaim the Gospel and bring about spiritual increase throughout the Roman empire.

The place to which God calls us may not be a desirable place in our own eyes. It may be a place that seems filled with difficulties and troubles—an alien, foreign, "hard" place in which to work, live, and worship.

The final place to which God called the apostle Paul was a prison in Rome. Few of us would consider that to be a worthy destination point for our lives or a place of increase, success, or honor. Yet it was from this prison chamber that Paul wrote a significant number of letters that became "books" of the New Testament. Paul had a powerful impact on the early church from that prison. Not only that, but he had the opportunity to win a number of highly placed Roman officers to the Lord. Paul's prison chamber was a place where he met with the Lord, proclaimed the Gospel, and wrote words that have brought edification to the people of God for nearly two thousand years!

The Lord also led the apostle John to a prison. His particular prison was remote—a cave on the barren, small island of Patmos. There John was cut off from the people he loved and the churches he had established. Was this God's place? Most definitely! It was there that God revealed Himself to John in a way that is perhaps the most profound revelation in all the Bible. God held John in the cleft of that barren rock on the side of Patmos and revealed to him the glory of the Lord.

When a place is the chosen place of God, it is always a place in which increase will be the result if we are diligent to obey the Lord.

The Journey to Your Place of Increase

You may not have arrived yet at the place God has for your increase. Rest assured, there *is* a place. God very likely is leading you step-by-step to that place of His ultimate outpouring into your life.

Long after Abraham's death, Isaac found himself living in an area south of Hebron, in the Negeb, when famine struck the land. (See Gen. 24:62.) Isaac headed toward the west with his herds and flocks, and entered the territory of Gerar, which was ruled by the Philistine king Abimelech. From there, the roads and trails followed by herdsmen led southward toward Egypt. In times of famine, the nomadic herdsmen of that region often took this southerly route toward Egypt where they fed their flocks and herds until the famine ended.

The Lord appeared to Isaac as he entered Gerar and said, "Do not go down to Egypt; live in the land of which I will tell you. Dwell temporarily in this land, and I will be with you and will favor you with blessings." (Gen. 26:2–3)

Isaac trusted in God and stayed in Gerar. From a natural standpoint, a *full* provision for his family, flocks, and herds lay in Egypt. There was no famine in Egypt—the grasslands were plentiful and the water abundant. Isaac chose, however, to trust in God rather than to trust in what natural circumstances seemed to dictate.

The Bible tells us that there in Gerar, which was intended to be a temporary place for Isaac, "Isaac sowed seed...and received in the same year a hundred times as much as he had planted, and the Lord favored him with blessings." (Gen. 26:12) In fact, in this temporary dwelling place, Isaac became "great and gained more and more until he became very wealthy and distinguished." (Gen. 26:13). With vast herds and flocks and a great many servants, Isaac became the envy of the Philistines and Abimelech finally asked him to leave, saying, "You are much mightier than we are." (Gen. 26:16)

Isaac went eastward to the Valley of Gerar and re-opened the wells which his father Abraham had dug and the Philistines had subsequently filled with earth. He gave to the wells the same names his father had given them. Isaac's servants also dug in the valley and found a well of living water—a natural spring. The herdsmen of Gerar quarreled with Isaac's herdsmen, laying claim to the new well. Isaac moved a little farther east and his servants dug another well. Again, the herdsmen of Gerar quarreled over it. Isaac moved his flocks and herds still farther east and his servants dug yet a third well. This time the Gerar herdsmen did not quarrel for it, and Isaac took this as a sign that he had finally moved far enough away from Abimelech that he and his family could live in peace.

He moved on to Beersheba, a little farther eastward, and there the Lord appeared to him and said, "I am the God of Abraham your father. Fear not, for I am with you and will favor you with blessings and multiply your descendants for the sake of My servant Abraham." (Gen. 26:24)

This was a sure sign to Isaac that he had finally arrived at the place where he would receive the fullness of God's blessings. Isaac built an altar and called on the name of the Lord and pitched his tent there. His servants again began to dig a well.

At this point Abimelech showed up with a trusted friend and the commander of the Philistine army. "And Isaac said to them, Why have you come to me, seeing that you hate me and have sent me away from you? They said, We saw that the Lord was certainly with you; so we said, Let there be now an oath between us...That you will do us no harm, inasmuch as we have not touched you and have done to you nothing but good and have sent you away in peace. You are now the blessed or favored of the Lord!" (Gen. 26:27-29)

What an admission for the king of a nation to make! Abimelech recognized that the hand of God was on Isaac and that God had blessed him with abundant increase. Isaac made a formal dinner for his guests and they ate and drank together. Then the next morning, they took oaths with one another and Isaac sent them on their way in peace. That same day, Isaac's servants told him that they had struck water. Isaac named the well Shibah, and the place became known as Beersheba—the well of the oath. Isaac had entered a land of plenty in which he could dwell in peace. He remained there the rest of his life.

Isn't that what we all long for—a land of plenty in which we can dwell in peace, even peace with those who have been our enemies or who have rejected us?

That is the exact place of ultimate increase that the Lord has for you. You may prosper materially in a land in which you are only to dwell temporarily. Your ultimate destination, however, is a place where you will prosper in all areas of your life and dwell in peace with God and your neighbors. Your ultimate destination is a place where the Lord appears to you and says, "Here I will favor you with blessings and multiply you."

Step by step, God moved Isaac into the exact position He wanted him to be. Step by step, God is also moving you into the exact position He wants you to occupy.

You May Encounter Obstacles. Along the way, you may encounter obstacles—Isaac certainly did. People may quarrel with you over your rights to the work you have done.

I can relate to Isaac in this area. More than twenty-seven years ago, God called me to go to a particular city. He said, "I am going to give you a voice in this city." I was young and ignorant at the time. It sounded good to me that I was going to have a voice in the city to which God had called me.

The Lord had neglected to tell me that when I stood up to speak, I was going to be sliced and diced. After that happened a few times, I found myself saying, "Jesus, let somebody else speak up and have a voice. I think I'll just come in on the afterglow. Let somebody else pave the way and I'll come in behind and be a good support person." That isn't what God had in mind. I still had to speak up.

Just because God calls you to do something does not mean that it is going to be easy or that you are going to experience immediate success.

Jonah was a prophet who knew about the difficulty of doing what God had asked him to do. Nineveh was a city that was sixty miles in circumference. It took a person three days to walk around that city. When Jonah went there, he had some walking to do. He had some crying out to do. He didn't encounter a reporter who could put him on the nightly news—he had to cry out personally, "Yet forty days and Nineveh shall be overthrown!" (Jonah 3:4)

The end result, however, was that the people of Nineveh believed Jonah, believed in God, proclaimed a fast, and put on sackcloth as a sign of their mourning. They turned away from their evil ways and their violence, and they cried out with a great voice to God for mercy.

Joshua was assured by the Lord that he and the Israelites were going to be victorious in their battles against the inhabitants of Canaan. He was given full assurance that God would fight the battle alongside the Israelites, and they would prevail and receive the full inheritance of the land that God had promised to them.

That does not mean, however, that God promised to give the land to them on a silver platter. Joshua and the Israelites still had to "possess" the land—to move into it, tread upon it, fight for it when necessary, subdue it, and occupy it. (See Josh. 1:3 and following.)

No place has ever been given to any believer as a gift tied with a bow. No place is handed over to believers overnight in full-blown conquest. In every instance in the Bible and throughout church history, we see that believers have had to move into territories occupied by evil forces and engage in the *process* of winning those territories for the Lord.

Moving into the place God has for you requires you to place your hand in the hand of the Lord and move forward, trusting God to help you do whatever is necessary to claim the place for Him.

In Isaac's case, the Lord did not require him to fight. Rather, He required him *not* to fight and simply to move on.

That's the advice Jesus gave to His disciples when He told them to make peace with their persecutors and to treat their enemies with kindness and generosity:

> Do not resist the evil man [who injures you];
> but if anyone strikes you on the right jaw or cheek,
> turn to him the other one, too.
> And if anyone wants to sue you and take your
> undershirt (tunic), let him have your coat also.
> And if anyone forces you to go one mile, go
> with him two [miles]. (Matt. 5:39–41)

If Jesus had been speaking to Isaac, He likely would have said, "Does anyone want the well you have dug? Give it to him and move on."

So many people spend countless hours haggling and wrangling over things they are certain are theirs. That same energy might be better used in letting go of what is disputed and moving on creatively, energetically, and wisely to engage in the next task that is one step further removed from a person who chooses to be an enemy.

Trust God to guide you step-by-step. At times He may ask you to speak up and make waves. At times He may call you to walk away. Trust God to lead you in the way He desires you to move. Trust Him to provide for you as you are obedient to His call. Trust Him to move you to the place of total provision.

Isaac may have lost a well or two, but there's no indication that he lost any of his wealth as he continued to move eastward away from Gerar.

You May Make Mistakes. Along the way, as God leads you, you may make mistakes. Isaac did. While he was in Gerar, Isaac deceived Abimelech, stating that his beautiful wife Rebekah was his sister. Isaac acted out of fear, thinking that the men of Gerar would kill him if they thought Rebekah was his wife. Abimelech discovered the truth and confronted Isaac, saying, "What is this you have done to us? One of the men might easily have lain with your wife, and you would have brought guilt and sin upon us." He then charged the people of Gerar, "He who touches this man or his wife shall surely be put to death." Even though Isaac lied, God spared him from evil consequences. (See Gen. 26:1-11.)

The good news for you today is that even if you have disobeyed God in the past, He will forgive you and can spare you evil consequences. Disobedience does not cancel out the ultimate eternal blessing God desires to give you. Disobedience may cause a delay in your receiving the fullness of God's blessing; disobedience may cause you to experience obstacles you wouldn't have otherwise experienced. But disobedience does not change

God's mind about who you are, what He has desired for you to do on this earth, or where He desires for you to spend eternity.

Ask God to forgive you. Turn back to the way God has commanded you to live. Pick up the call that God has placed on your life. Begin to do what God has gifted you to do. And watch how God begins to bless your life.

I once read a story about a young man who became involved in Satan worship as a teenager. He became so deeply involved with the occult that by all biblical definitions, he became possessed by demons. In a fit of hatred and anger, this young man brutally murdered his parents. He was tried in a court of law and sentenced to death for his crime.

Did this young man's extreme disobedience cancel out the blessing God desired for him? No. God did not change His mind about this young man. He did not love him less. He did not cancel out all of the good things He had planned for him from the foundation of the earth.

While this young man was in prison awaiting his death sentence, he encountered people who loved him and who shared with him the Gospel of Jesus Christ. He responded to their message and gave his heart to the Lord. Almost immediately, he began to read and study the Word of God and to witness to others who were on death row with him. He began to write letters to people outside the prison, encouraging them to confess their sins and accept Jesus as their Savior and Lord. He began to use his talents for the Lord's work, and eventually he wrote a book about his experience and about the goodness of God.

Was it God's plan that this young man accept Jesus as his Savior? Yes. Was it God's plan that this young man turn his life around and live in accordance with God's commandments? Yes.

Was it God's plan that this young man witness to others and become a soul winner? Absolutely. Was it God's plan that he use his talents for the furtherance of God's Kingdom? Yes.

Was it God's plan that this young man eventually receive eternal life in Christ Jesus? Absolutely. And the moment this young man was executed for his crime, Jesus received him into glory. That young man has a heavenly home and eternal life.

Certainly, it was not God's desire that this young man kill his parents or experience prison. This teenager's willful disobedience and rebellion against God's laws resulted in negative earthly consequences. Furthermore, his acceptance of Jesus Christ did nothing to nullify that earthly consequence. God allowed this young man to be put to death for his crime.

What this young man's salvation meant, however, was a complete nullification of any *eternal* consequences Satan had intended. His acceptance of Christ Jesus meant that his spirit would live forever and that his ultimate purpose on this earth was fulfilled: to accept Christ, to grow in faith and in knowledge of God's Word, and to extend the Kingdom of God.

No matter how heinous your disobedience, God still holds out to you the promise of eternal life if you will confess your sins and receive Jesus Christ as your Savior and Lord. If you have sinned as a Christian, turn again to Christ Jesus and ask His forgiveness and His cleansing. The Bible tells us, "If we [freely] admit that we have sinned and confess our sins, He is faithful and just (true to His own nature and promises) and will forgive our sins [dismiss our lawlessness] and [continuously] cleanse us from all unrighteousness [everything not in conformity to His will in purpose, thought, and action]." (I John 1:9)

The danger is when we refuse to own up to our sins or try to justify our sins. That is what keeps us from forgiveness.

In many cases throughout the Bible, we also find that God reverses negative consequences that we experience as a result of our sin. Jacob ran to the home of his uncle Laban after tricking his brother Esau out of his birthright and blessing. While he was there and as he returned, Jacob experienced a great time of renewal in the Lord. The negative consequences that Jacob feared were reversed.

Moses ran to Midian to escape the wrath of Pharaoh after Moses killed an Egyptian whom he witnessed abusing a Hebrew man. Moses lived in the desert for forty years, but then he had a divine encounter with the living God. The Lord reversed the negative consequences in his life and used him mightily to bring deliverance to his people.

Trust God to reverse the negative consequences that your sin may have brought upon your life. The prophet Joel encouraged the people of God to trust God to reverse the evil consequences under which they were living:

> Rend your hearts...and return to the Lord, your God, for He is gracious and merciful, slow to anger, and abounding in loving-kindness; and He revokes His sentence of evil [when His conditions are met].

> Who knows but what He will turn, revoke your sentence [of evil], and leave a blessing behind Him [giving you the means with which to serve Him]...? (Joel 2:13–14)

Our prayer must continually be, "Have mercy on me, Lord."

Your Journey May Take Years

The Lord may require you to "travel" for years before you arrive at your place.

It took Joseph thirteen years to get to his final place of increase.

It took David about seventeen years to get to his place of increase.

It took the children of Israel about four hundred and seventy-five years to get to the Promise Land.

Refuse to be discouraged if you seem to have been on a journey to your promised place of increase for many years and have not yet arrived. Continue to submit your life to the Lord. Continue to trust God to bring you into the fullness of all He has planned for you.

Take confidence in this truth: The only reason that God puts any person in a specific place is for the benefit of the Kingdom of God. You are placed in a specific opportunity, calling, community, church, and circle of family and friends so that you might be fruitful there *for the benefit of God's plan and purpose on this earth.*

Move In and Settle Down

When you arrive at the place God intends for you to experience increase, you must tread upon it and claim it. You must subdue it, dominate it, and possess it. You must "move in" and "settle" the house, the land, the business, the church, the ministry, or the territory God has given you authority over.

God did not place Adam and Eve in the Garden of Eden and say to them, "Enjoy yourselves. Have a good time." No. He said to them, "*You* take care of the garden. *You take care of your place.* Subdue it. Tend it. Guard it. Keep it." (See Gen. 2:15.)

The more you are fruitful in the place God has prepared for you, the greater the blessing and multiplication you will experience.

Plant yourself. Put down roots. Begin to exercise the spiritual gifts God has given you. Find a niche in which there are needs that you are uniquely equipped and called to meet with God's help. Find God's "room" carved out for you to occupy. And then, stay there.

Don't wander from church to church, group to group. Give in as many ways as you find to give of yourself—give of your resources, your time, your natural talent, your spiritual gifts, your skills, your wisdom. Get involved. *Cultivate* what you plant and raise it up for the glory of God.

The more you are fruitful in the place God has prepared for you, the greater the blessing and multiplication you will experience.

A Place of Peace

Ultimately, the place to which God leads you is a place of peace—deep, inner calm, assurance, and confidence. God's peace

includes feelings of purpose, satisfaction, and fulfillment. To be
at peace means to enter the kind of contentment described by the
apostle Paul when he wrote to the Philippians,

> I know how to be abased and live humbly in
> straitened circumstances, and I know also how to
> enjoy plenty and live in abundance. I have learned
> in any and all circumstances the secret of facing
> every situation, whether well-fed or going hungry,
> having a sufficiency and enough to spare or going
> without and being in want. (Phil. 4:12)

Peace does not mean that you will live in peace with every
person or that the devil will stop harassing you. Isaac was able to
live in peace with his neighbors, but that does not mean that his
entire life was marked by peace. Far from it! His own two sons,
Jacob and Esau, made his life anything but peaceful at the end as
they disputed over matters such as birthright and blessing. (See
Gen. 27–28.)

Peace is inner, and it is based upon one's relationship with
the Lord. It is not external—or rooted in relationships we have
with other people. Jesus made it very clear to his disciples that
they would face difficult external times in life,

> I have told you these things, so that in Me you
> may have [perfect] peace and confidence. In the
> world you have tribulation and trials and distress
> and frustration; but be of good cheer [take courage;
> be confident, certain, undaunted]! For I have
> overcome the world. [I have deprived it of power
> to harm you and have conquered it for you.] (John
> 16:33)

Persecution from those who oppose the Gospel—either
knowingly or unknowingly—is a part of the Christian life, no
matter how much increase you may experience. Many people
seem to believe that if they increase to a certain level, they will

rise above any persecution regarding what they say or do. That simply isn't what the Bible teaches.

Very often, persecution escalates the more we experience God's increase. Jesus certainly indicated this to be true as He taught His disciples in the aftermath of an encounter He had one day with a rich man who asked, "What must I do to inherit eternal life?" (Mark 10:17)

Jesus knew that this man was trusting in his riches more than he was trusting in God, and He said to him, "You lack one thing; go and sell all you have and give [the money] to the poor, and you will have treasure in heaven; and come [and] accompany Me [walking the same road that I walk]." (Mark 10:21)

Upon hearing that, the man's countenance fell and he went away grieved and sorrowing. He could not bring himself to part with his wealth. He preferred to trust in it and pursue matters related to it, rather than trust in God fully to provide for him.

God requires of us that we not *trust* in increase, rather that we place all of our trust in the Lord who gives the increase. We are never to trust in money or wealth, rather to trust in the Lord who is the Source of all riches.

Jesus said about this rich man after he had departed, "It is easier for a camel to go through the eye of a needle than for a rich man to enter the kingdom of God." (Mark 10:25)

His disciples were shocked at this and replied, "Then who can be saved?" Jesus said, "With men [it is] impossible, but not with God; for all things are possible with God." (Mark 10:26-27) Jesus made it very clear that no person can purchase salvation and no person can "earn" his way into favor with God. God is the One who extends salvation to all who will receive it. No man has ever "increased" to the point of gaining salvation or of being worthy of salvation. Neither has any person ever increased himself to the point where he does not need salvation!

Peter followed up this statement from Jesus by saying, "We have yielded up and abandoned everything [once and for all and joined You as Your disciples, siding with Your party] and accompanied You [walking the same road that You walk]." (Mark 10:28)

Let me remind you that Peter was a successful businessman at the time he met Jesus and began to follow Him. Biblical historians believe he may have owned as many as six or seven boats that fished the Galilee. He had a large home in Capernaum. He gave it all up to follow Jesus.

You can almost hear the question in his voice, "What will be our reward?" Jesus answered,

> Truly I tell you, there is no one who has given up and left house or brothers or sisters or mother or father or children or lands for My sake and for the Gospel's
> Who will not receive a hundred times as much now in this time—houses and brothers and sisters and mothers and children and lands, with persecutions—and in the age to come, eternal life.
> But many [who are now] first will be last [then], and many [who are now] last will be first [then]. (Mark 10:29-31)

I'm sure Peter was thrilled at the thought that he and the other disciples would be receiving a hundredfold in their earthly lives and then receiving eternal life at death. But notice that little phrase tucked into the promise of a hundredfold increase: *with persecutions.*

The more you are blessed, the more the devil is going to do everything in his power to steal from you and to destroy you. (See John 10:10.)

The more you are blessed, the more certain people are going to be jealous of you.

The more you are blessed, the higher your profile in the community and the more subject you are going to be to public scrutiny and criticism.

Several years ago I went to a meeting with various ministers from different denominations. A well-known minister in our city came to the meeting. He pulled into the parking lot about the same time I did, driving his 1962 Chevrolet. I was driving a late-model Cadillac.

I felt a little intimidated. I left the meeting early so nobody would see what kind of vehicle I was driving. As I left the meeting, I thought, *Now I know why some people do not understand God's blessings. Some people are looking at material things as a sign of a person's humility before God. Other people are looking at material things as a sign that a person is bragging or proud.*

Material possessions are not a sign of *anything*—neither blessing nor cursing.

We need to ask ourselves, "Who are we trying to impress? Who are we trying to convince about our blessing or our humility?"

If we are really honest with ourselves, the answer very often lies in our own mirror. In many cases, the answer also involves the opinions of others. The real questions are these, "What does *God* say? What does *God* promise?" God is the only one we should be trying to please. He is the One who knows our hearts, our motives, our desires, and our ambitions.

God promises increase to those who abide by His commandments, trust in Him with a whole heart, and give of themselves in faith. We should never be ashamed of the increase He sends our way. At the same time, we need to be diligent in using that increase in the ways He desires!

The Ultimate Place God Has for Us

Jesus said to those who followed Him, "In My Father's house there are many dwelling places (homes). If it were not so, I would have told you; for I am going away to prepare a place for you. And when (if) I go and make ready a place for you, I will come back again and will take you to Myself, that where I am you may be also." (John 14:2–3)

Jesus promised us a place—and more importantly, a place in which we would be *with Him.* Our place in eternity is close to Jesus—so close that wherever He is, there we are also.

The world seeks a "place in the sun."

God has a place for you in the eternal Son. There is a place for you in Christ Jesus!

The place God has prepared for us is a very large place. The city of Heaven is calculated in the Book of Revelation as being fifteen hundred miles long, wide, and high. It is made of pure transparent gold. The foundation, walls, and gates are of precious stones. Light fills and radiates from this city, and everything in it is marked by splendor and majesty.

Any time you become discouraged that you might not yet be in the place of increase that God has for you, remind yourself of the glories that lie ahead in your heavenly home. That is your ultimate destination point—and the place of your ultimate increase!

Chapter 13

Challenges on the Way to Increase

Why do we fail to experience increase in the land to which the Lord calls us?

First, many people have a false understanding about what is required to possess something the Lord has promised to them. There is a *process* between promise and possession. Increase doesn't happen overnight.

Life increase is not magical. It doesn't come by making a one-time offering to the Lord on Sunday morning so that a miracle arrives in the mailbox by Tuesday noon.

Life increase is not mystical. It doesn't fall out of heaven in neatly labeled boxes that land in a person's front yard.

Life increase is a process in which man works alongside God to *do* what God commands with faith that God will provide and protect and empower.

Second, many people do not recognize the spiritual forces that are amassed against them. You are going to experience assaults against your assigned place in God's Kingdom. Some of those assaults are going to come from the devil and his demons. Some will come from the world and the world's systems. Some may even come from those in your own family and circle of friends who claim they are operating in your best interests.

Why do we experience these assaults if our intent and motivation is to do what is right and to extend the Kingdom of God? Because the devil does not want God's Kingdom established, enlarged, enriched, or expanded! His warfare is not solely against you, rather it is against God's plan and purpose for your life. He wants to see you fail miserably at the tasks the Lord has placed before you so that the Lord will receive less of the glory and honor due His name!

When you are facing a spiritual battle, put on the whole armor that God has provided for you and begin to pray. (See Eph. 6:11–18.)

Third, many people simply give up when they realize that conflict or hard work or spiritual warfare may be involved in the taking possession of what God has promised. So many people allow themselves to be swallowed up by circumstances, adversity, or rejection. They throw up their hands in defeat and refuse to press forward and trust God to open the way.

If the children of Israel had given up when they reached the Red Sea and returned to Egypt, they not only would have been put back into slavery, but they would likely have experienced even greater hardship from their taskmasters.

If Joseph had used his position of authority in Egypt to hire a chariot and return to his family in Canaan, he very likely would have found himself in a position of starvation and begging right along with them.

If Jonah had not finally said yes to the Lord and gone to Ninevah, thousands upon thousands of people would have died without having been given the opportunity to repent and turn to the Lord.

When you begin to take steps toward the place of increase that God has promised to you, *expect* challenges to arise. In fact, you should probably expect everything to go wrong that can go wrong! The enemy will do his utmost to keep you from occupying fully the place God has for you. Some of the assault may come in the form of oppression, depression, or discouragement. Some of it may be manifested through people who choose to become outright enemies.

Some of it may be manifested in "systems" of various types that seem suddenly to work against you—equipment that breaks, transportation systems that fail, computers that develop glitches, bureaucratic wheels that seem to turn even slower than usual, forms that get lost, and countless other functions that break down.

I don't know where Christians got the idea that God had promised them a rose garden, with all of the roses producing everlasting blooms and growing without cultivation, without a need to control aphids and other pests, without a need for fertilization and pruning, and without thorns! That simply isn't the reality of this world! God may have promised us a rose garden but, if so, He also has equipped us to be good gardeners and empowered us to do the work necessary for producing roses that will bring Him glory.

Don't Let Defeat Define Your Life

The story of Joseph is one of the most amazing stories in the Old Testament. Joseph was a man who refused to accept defeat in his life. He never ceased to be challenged by the dreams that God gave to him as a young man. He never ceased to see himself as a man worthy of wearing the tunic given to him by his father. (See Gen. 37.)

The tunic given to Joseph has been described by Bible scholars as a tunic of "palms and soles." It reached past his wrists and ankles. The normal tunic for a man was sleeveless and was about knee-length. Long, flowing tunics with long sleeves were worn by princes, rulers, and those who were wealthy enough not to have to engage in manual labor. This tunic was a strong sign to Joseph that God had a destiny of rulership, leadership, and authority for him. Joseph knew in his heart that God had a great purpose and plan for his life. He lived with that attitude and belief, and apparently he wasn't shy in sharing his attitude with his brothers. They mocked him for his attitude and were jealous of him.

In their jealousy, Joseph's brothers sold him to a band of gypsy-like traders. They sold him for even *less* than the price of an average slave, adding insult to injury.

Joseph was then sold by these traders to Potiphar, an influential Egyptian, an officer of Pharaoh, and captain and chief executioner of the royal guard.

Joseph continued to operate in his gifting and he became a successful and prosperous man even as a slave in this Egyptian's house. He eventually was made supervisor over all that Potiphar owned—both his house and his fields. Joseph continued to operate in righteousness, refusing to compromise his morals even though he was tempted repeatedly by Potiphar's wife to engage in an adulterous affair. Joseph may have been a slave according to his outward circumstances, but he was never *enslaved* in his mind and heart.

Joseph *increased* in Potiphar's house, and under his leadership Potiphar's household also increased.

Joseph was thrown into the state prison when Potiphar's wife falsely accused him. This prison was undoubtedly the worst dungeon in the land. Prisoners who were sent there were usually given a very harsh sentence—either execution or life without parole. Read what the Scriptures say about Joseph in this place:

> But the Lord was with Joseph, and showed him mercy and loving-kindness and gave him favor in the sight of the warden of the prison.
>
> And the warden of the prison committed to Joseph's care all the prisoners who were in the prison; and whatsoever was done there, he was in charge of it.
>
> The prison warden paid no attention to anything that was in [Joseph's] charge, for the Lord was with him and made whatever he did to prosper. (Gen. 39:21–23)

Your prison may be a bad marriage. It may be bankruptcy. It may be a disease the doctors have said is terminal. My word to you is this, "The Lord is with you!" And when the Lord is with you, you are in position to receive mercy and loving-kindness! You are in a position to prosper!

Did Joseph give up on God's call on his life? No. Joseph had the attitude, "Devil, you may have knocked me down, but you haven't knocked me out."

Joseph continued to function in the fullness of his gifts, and the warden of the prison eventually committed to Joseph's care all of the prisoners in the prison. He continued to function as a manager and a leader. The result was that Joseph prospered in everything he did. He may have been a prisoner, but he was never imprisoned in his mind and heart!

The story is told of a little boy who misbehaved repeatedly until finally his mother said to him, "Johnny, you go stand in that corner and stay there until I tell you that you can leave."

Johnny went to stand in the corner. His mother returned a few minutes later and found Johnny standing there, grinning from ear to ear. She said, "Why are you grinning?" He said, "I may be standing in this corner on the outside, but on the inside I'm sittin' down."

That was the attitude of Joseph. He may have been in prison, but he wasn't thinking like a prisoner—he was thinking like a man in charge of the prison. He may have been standing up and working diligently on the outside, but on the inside he was sitting down on a throne of authority!

Joseph refused to let anyone take away his dream or his relationship with God.

If God allows you to be in a difficult situation, He has you there for a purpose. He is using that situation to refine something in you or provide you with an opportunity to serve others.

What God has placed in you, no person can take away from you. The devil cannot steal it away. Nothing and no one can compromise who God has said you are or what God has declared over your life. You, and only you, can shelf that dream or compromise God's purpose for you. In like manner, you, and only you, can choose to hold on to your dream and refuse to let go of all that God has placed in you, designed for you, or done on your behalf.

It was while he was in prison that Joseph encountered the king's baker and butler. Both were accused of being part of an overthrow plot against Pharaoh. Each of these men had a dream while in prison. When Joseph came to these men the morning after their dreams, he "looked at them" and "saw that they were sad and depressed." He asked these servants of Pharaoh, "Why do you look so dejected and sad today?" (See Gen. 40:6–7.)

What an amazing man Joseph is! He's in prison himself. Every man in that prison has good cause to be sad and depressed. Joseph himself probably has the greatest reason to be sad and depressed. He refuses to adopt that identity and demeanor, however. Joseph is sensitive and perceptive to the needs of others around him. He considers his location and situation to be temporary.

How do I know that Joseph did not consider this prison to be his permanent home? Because after Joseph had interpreted the dreams of the butler, he said to him, "Think of me when it shall be well with you, and show kindness, I beg of you, to me, and mention me to Pharaoh and get me out of this house." (Gen. 40:14)

Joseph continued to hold on to his dream and to his relationship with the Lord. And out of the core of a character defined by God, he expressed *care* for those over whom he was given responsibility.

Is it any wonder that a man who managed others with this degree of concern would be able to get the maximum amount of work and loyalty out of them so that things under his management flowed smoothly?

If God allows you to be in a difficult situation, He has you there for a purpose. He is using that situation to refine something

---

Don't let the world interpret your dream. Don't let the world or any forces of evil define you, predict your future, or give you your identity.

---

in you or provide you with an opportunity to serve others. Keep your eyes on the *permanent* goals God has for you. Hold on to the ultimate reward and position He has promised you!

Several years ago our daughter Melony said to me, "Dad, I need to get to the position where I am no longer pre-occupied with the idea of getting married. I want to have my mind pre-occupied with what the Lord is calling me to do. I want to love the Lord and be sold out to Him. I want to be totally consumed with doing what the Lord is calling me to do and then do that with all my heart."

I said to her, "Melony, if you can get to that place, you will realize your destiny. You will be precisely where the Lord wants you so He can bring about His best for your life."

Are you allowing some earthly, temporary situation to keep you from being totally sold out to the Lord? Are you using something as an excuse for *not* doing the very things that you know the Lord has called you to do?

The baker and butler said to Joseph, "We have dreamed dreams, and there is no one to interpret them." Joseph replied, "Do not interpretations belong to God?" (Gen. 40:8)

What an incredible response Joseph made! Do not interpretations of all dreams belong to God—including the interpretation of *your* dream? Don't let the world interpret your dream. Don't let the world or any forces of evil define you, predict your future, or give you your identity. The dreams and hopes God has placed in your heart should be interpreted *only* in the light of God's Word!

When Pharaoh dreamed a dream for which his advisors had no interpretation, the butler—who was restored to his position as the king's cup bearer—remembered that Joseph had interpreted his dream and he recommended that Pharaoh call upon Joseph.

At first reading, you may assume that the destiny of Joseph was placed into the hands of a butler. Nothing could be farther from the truth. Two years had passed between the time Joseph interpreted the butler's dream and the day that Pharaoh sent for him. People may play a *part* in bringing about the fulfillment of your dream, but your destiny lies solely in the hands of God. God's timing is precise; His methods are perfect.

When Pharaoh told his dream to Joseph, Joseph replied, "It is not in me; God [not I] will give Pharaoh a [favorable] answer of peace." (Gen. 41:16)

Joseph was only one divine revelation away from a complete change in his circumstances. You may be in that same position today. Circumstances and conditions can change very quickly; nothing can stand in God's way when God chooses to act. Our part is not to predict *when* God may move on our behalf, rather to be ready to act decisively, boldly, and with total reliance upon the Lord when that moment comes. Joseph did not attempt to interpret Pharaoh's dream in his own strength and power. He relied completely upon the Lord to give him the interpretation. Once that interpretation came, he did not hesitate to deliver it.

Trust God to give you the guidance you need—ask Him for it and rely on Him to answer your prayer. And then, when His guidance becomes clear...move out, speak out, take action. Do what it is the Lord reveals to you to do!

When Trouble Turns into Persecution

At times, God has used rather severe measures to *move* His people into the position where He intends for them to be fruitful and to experience increase. In a number of places in the Old Testament, we find that when God desired to get the attention of the Israelites, He shut down their economy—He brought about failure in the barter system, He brought about a devaluation of their money system, or He brought about drought that resulted in a failure to produce crops. At other times, the Lord allowed His people to be persecuted for their faith.

We tend to regard persecution as a negative. But from God's perspective, it can be a great positive. Persecution is one means God uses to move His people into the place where He desires for them to plant their lives.

Joseph certainly experienced suffering, sorrow, and persecution in being uprooted from his home and plunked down in a slave's position in Egypt.

Suffering and persecution were also involved in God's moving of His people out of Egypt four centuries later. The ten plagues that came upon Egypt were far from pleasant. Those plagues were not only intended to move Pharaoh's heart to let God's people go from their positions as slaves—they were also intended to prepare the hearts of the Israelites so they would *want* to leave the place and the routines to which they had become accustomed.

The Israelites had been in Egypt for four hundred years. Their daily lives as slaves may have been hard, but they had grown accustomed to life in Egypt. They had built homes and communities, raised families, and put down deep roots. To venture out of Egypt was a huge endeavor—monumental change was involved of the deepest nature. To leave Egypt meant a complete upside-down turning of their lives.

In the months that followed the resurrection and ascension of Jesus, the church took root in Jerusalem. The believers shared a common life together—sharing meals and celebrating their faith on a daily basis. However, a small band of believers in Jerusalem was not God's idea of how great and far-reaching His church should be!

Death-dealing persecution drove believers out of Jerusalem so the Gospel might be extended to communities across Judea and Samaria, and even into Syria and Ethiopia. Persecution drove the apostle Peter to Caesarea, and from there to the house of Cornelius, so the Gospel might be extended to the Gentile world. Persecution was a major factor in the missionary journeys of Paul.

It was often a mob riot or an instance of suffering that drove Paul from one city to the next, all so the Gospel might be extended throughout the Roman world.

The Book of Acts is largely a book of persecution and suffering as the Gospel spread across the Roman empire. In cities from Rome to Alexandria, the church began to take root and be fruitful— to flourish, to expand, to *increase*.

Be Quick to Obey

When you find yourself in a position of trouble or persecution, quickly ask God, "What are You trying to teach me? Where are You trying to lead me?" Search for His answers. Listen to His voice. And when He directs you, be quick to move. Never try to avoid God's call to move in a particular direction.

Jonah knew the consequences of trying to escape God's call.

Jonah was a prophet. Many Bible scholars believe he not only was the subject of the Book of Jonah, but that he was the prophet identified in II Kings 14:25 as Jonah son of Amittai. Jonah had prophesied that King Jeroboam II would enlarge the northern borders of Israel, regaining territory that King Hazael of Syria had taken earlier. The fulfillment of this prophecy gave Jonah strong credentials as a prophet and he no doubt felt that the Lord was going to use him in great ways.

Then the Lord spoke to Jonah to go to Nineveh, one of the foremost cities in Assyria. The Assyrians hated the Israelites and were extremely cruel to them. They were preparing a major assault against Israel. The Israelites, in turn, hated the Assyrians and were very fearful of them. The Ninevites were the last people on earth that Jonah wanted to see as responding to God or being shown leniency by God.

Jonah refused to go to Nineveh and he engaged in a power struggle with God. He ran to Joppa and boarded a ship headed for Tarshish, which was in the area now known as Spain. Tarshish was in the opposite direction of Nineveh, about a year's sailing away from Joppa. Jonah was desperate to get away from God's call and to get as far away from Nineveh as possible.

As we know from the Book of Jonah, Jonah found himself on a ship that encountered a violent tempest. The ship was about to break up, and suspicion was cast on Jonah who admitted to the sailors that he was running away from God. He advised them to throw him overboard, which they did not initially want to do but which they eventually did. The sea immediately became calm once Jonah was thrown overboard, which caused these sailors to reverently and worshipfully fear the Lord, offer a sacrifice to the Lord, and make vows to Him. Jonah had a profound impact on those sailors even in his disobedience!

For his part, Jonah was swallowed up by a great fish that the Lord had "prepared and appointed." I don't know what kind of fish that was, but I do know this—the Bible says the Lord prepared it and appointed it, and it swallowed up Jonah.

You may run from God. You may fail God miserably. You may be at the worst point in your life. But know this—God sees you, loves you, and still has a plan and purpose for your life. No matter how much you may abandon God, He never abandons you. You are never beyond His reach.

The psalmist assures us,

> If I ascend up into heaven, You are there; if I make my bed in Sheol (the place of the dead), behold, You are there.
> If I take the wings of the morning or dwell in the uttermost parts of the sea,
> Even there shall Your hand lead me, and Your right hand shall hold me.
> If I say, Surely the darkness shall cover me and the night shall be [the only] light about me,
> Even the darkness hides nothing from You, but the night shines as the day. (Ps. 139:8–12)

There, in the belly of a great fish, Jonah finally prayed to the Lord and agreed to fulfill God's prophetic call on his life. No sooner had Jonah said "yes" to God than God spoke to the fish to vomit Jonah upon dry land.

Jonah's rescue is not merely the story of the saving of a prophet from drowning but, ultimately, the saving of a great city that was drowning in sin. Jonah went to Nineveh and proclaimed God's Word, and the people repented. Thousands upon thousands of people were spared from destruction. Jonah had the greatest revival meeting of his entire life in Nineveh. It was a place of great multiplication.

Don't let fear keep you from acting on what God commands you to do.

I have met people who are afraid that if they surrender their lives to God, He will call them to go to Africa and work as missionaries. Let me assure you, if God calls you to Africa to work as a missionary, that work in Africa will be the most wonderful, purposeful, and blessed work you will ever know. God does not call you to a place for failure. He calls you to a place so you might succeed in the work He has for you and to be blessed in the process of doing that work!

You can either run from God...or run with God. To run with God is the best of all worlds. When you run with God, your strides become so easy it is as if you have been set on cruise control. There is a force and a power undergirding you. The wind is at your back, the way is open in front of you, and nothing can impede your progress.

God desires to get the greatest glory possible from your life. The greatest glory He can get from your life is directly related to your obedience. If you hinder God's work in you, through you, and around you, you are going to diminish the glory God receives from your life.

Pray in Your Times of Trouble

Above all, pray in your times of trouble, suffering, and persecution. That is the most effective and important thing you can do! I learned that fact from my mother, who taught me about prayer by her example.

My father was an alcoholic and during his drinking binges, he was often away from home for weeks at a time. During those times, my mother would literally "pray in" groceries. She would pray and we would come home to find bags of groceries on our porch, never knowing who had left them.

One time when my father was away for nine weeks, people began to tell us that he must have died. My mother had all of us children get down on our knees to join her in prayer. She got up from that prayer time saying, "No, he's not dead. We need to go find him." The first place we looked, we found him. He had been in that place for nine weeks in a drunken stupor.

You can either run from God...or run with God. To run with God is the best of all worlds.

Prayer was the rhythm of my mother's life. Mom believed that a person should tell God every detail of their life. Prayer was a time for pouring out to God everything a person felt— from joy to pain—and for telling God all that had happened, all that was happening, and all that one desired to have happen.

My mother believed that prayer and faith were the means for receiving an *answer* to everything. Mom believed that if you prayed and had faith, you had done your part. Everything else was up to God. If you received what you asked for, God gave it. If you didn't receive what you prayed for, God had said "no."

My mother believed that a person had to trust God minute by minute, hour by hour. She believed there was nothing that God could not handle if we were faithful.

One time the boss at the mill came to my mother and said, "I've just had word that there are probably going to be some lay-offs at the mill in the near future. I want you to agree with me to pray. I've noticed that when you pray, things happen."

My mother replied, "What should I be praying about?"

He said, "I don't want to have to lay people off."

My mother said, "Well, then we need to pray that the company does more business and gets more orders for our cloth."

He nodded. And then she did something he wasn't expecting. She took his hand, and right there between the looms she started praying. It wasn't an elaborate prayer. But I can guarantee you it was direct and it was powerful.

Several days later, my mother came home and announced to us, "I'm going to have to work on Saturdays."

I didn't want her to have to work that hard and I started protesting. She interrupted me, "No, I *want* to work. This is a blessing. The boss came by today and told me that the company has had so many orders that the mill is going to have to start running a shift on Saturdays, and we might even have to run two shifts on Saturdays. Business has really picked up."

There were no lay-offs as anticipated, instead there was overtime pay.

The Lord has ways of moving mountains to meet your needs. He will even bless heathen companies to provide for you.

Prayer and obedience can do a great deal to cut short a period of struggle, trauma, persecution, or trial. When you find yourself forced to your knees by overwhelming trouble, use that time on your knees for prayer!

And remember always: In the midst of your distress, God still desires to increase *you*. Trust Him to do in you a work that He ultimately will manifest around you.

Chapter 14

Enlargement after Sacrifice

Every person faces a major trial or point of testing in their life. A number of smaller trials may come prior to the "big test." These generally help us prepare for that moment in which our faith and obedience will be tested. Before the final outpouring of increase, however, a person generally must face a *major* trial of their faith.

Generally speaking, the testing period in a person's life begins soon after a person receives and begins to act in faith on a promise from the Lord. The enemy of our souls seems to do his utmost to nip a promise in the bud rather than let it flourish in our souls.

The test may come in the form of numerous challenges or troubles—internal or external. We may find ourselves in inner turmoil, struggling with doubt, discouragement, or feelings of failure and unworthiness. We may find ourselves battling external forces that bring about some type of loss or disruption in our lives. The test may come in the form of disappointing news, rejection or alienation from people, or actions against us intended to diminish us or destroy our reputation.

The net effect of a test is a determination as to whether we are going to receive and then act upon the promise of God in our lives. Countless promises from God have gone unfulfilled because those who heard the promise refused to believe the promise and act on it. They allowed the words of the promise to evaporate in their souls. Or they allowed the time of testing to completely overshadow the promise to the point of obliteration.

If we are going to receive the fulfillment of God's promise in our lives, we *must* continue to trust God, regardless of the nature or severity of a test. We must refuse to give in to the temptation to abandon all hope of the promise becoming a visible reality in our lives.

The testing period generally culminates in a major show-down of some type. As part of that final test, a form of sacrifice is required.

A sacrifice refers to the laying down, putting aside, or submitting of something. The sacrifice may be to set aside our insistence upon proof or our strict adherence to doing or believing only those things that seem "reasonable." It may be a requirement that we lay down our own pride and self-reliance. It may be a requirement that we lay aside all doubt. It may be that we need to submit our creativity, time, resources, or some other aspect of our life. It may be that we need to submit our will to God's authority or to a person God has placed in authority over us.

At still other times, we must sacrifice certain activities in our lives in order to bring ourselves, our schedules, and our possessions into position to receive God's promise.

Many people routinely engage in things that are totally extraneous to what God desires for their lives. They aren't necessarily sinning—they simply are putting their time and money into things that will never bear eternal fruit. They are wasting the resources God has given them, while still expecting God to give them more resources. They are squandering time, all the while

---

Before the final outpouring of
increase, however, a person
generally must face a major trial
of their faith.

---

hoping and believing that God will make them more productive and effective. God's required sacrifice from you may be the giving up of a hobby, a club membership, a regularly scheduled game, or an idle pastime so you can devote more of your time, mental energy, and resources into those things that are directly related to the call of God on your life.

No matter what trial you undergo, and no matter what God asks you to sacrifice to Him, cling to the truth that God is *using* that sacrifice-related test to put you into a position to receive His highest and best blessings.

God's Enlargement Process

God's Word is very clear on this subject. Difficult seasons come into our lives as part of God's enlargement process.

For a number of years, perhaps as long as a decade, David experienced great difficulty. King Saul was seeking to kill him and David was literally "on the run," moving frequently with the band of men who had associated themselves with him. During that time, he sang in anguish to the Lord: "The troubles of my heart have enlarged; Oh, bring me out of my distresses!" (Ps. 25:17 NKJV)

David's enlarged troubles, however, had a perfecting and "enlarging" work in his heart. We read in Psalm 4:1—"Answer me when I call, O God of my righteousness (uprightness, justice and right standing with You)! You have freed me when I was hemmed in and enlarged me when I was in distress; have mercy upon me and hear my prayer."

Enlarged troubles can lead to an enlargement of *you.*

The Enlargement of Your Life

Do you truly want to be *everything* God has designed you to be? Do you want to accomplish all that God desires for you to do in your life? Do you want to maximize your potential and reach your highest goals? Do you want your life to have the greatest amount of meaning, purpose, and satisfaction possible? Do you want to be one hundred percent successful in your Christian walk?

If you answer yes to those questions, I have a little piece of bad news for you. You are going to experience enlarged troubles. Some of those troubles may come in the form of greater pressures on your time, a higher learning curve, a seemingly insurmountable goal, or an increase in stress.

Enlarged troubles can lead to an enlargement of you.

Before you panic, however, let me share a great deal of *good* news. Your enlarged troubles are going to bring you to a place of inner enlargement.

The success that lies ahead for you is going to require an enlargement of far more than your bank account or your financial portfolio. It's going to require an enlargement of your *person*. Your character, reputation, integrity, and maturity must enlarge so that you have the capacity and capability for handling the success God desires for you.

Now enlarged troubles do not automatically increase us. At times they can decrease us *if we choose to give up our hope and wallow in them.* If we choose to do things our way (no longer living in humility before the Lord), choose to go our own way (no longer following God's directives), or choose to trust in our own resources (no longer trusting fully in God's provision), we put ourselves into a "decrease" position. That is not what God desires for us, but it is what He allows to happen if we willfully choose any path other than His or place our trust in anything or any person other than Him. The purpose of God for our troubles, struggles, suffering, and sorrow is not to decrease us, but to increase us.

King Saul lost his kingship, his anointing, and ultimately his life because he did not respond to times of challenge in accordance with God's commandments. Saul moved *away* from God in a time of challenge and he was greatly *decreased* as a result.

King David, in contrast, moved *toward* God in his time of challenge. He submitted his life in humility to the Lord, put all of his trust in God, and chose to obey God regardless of his circumstances or the pressures of people around him. David was enlarged in his time of distress.

A Place of Enlargement

David's enlargement led him to a *place* of enlargement. In Psalm 18:18–20 we read:

> They confronted and came upon me in the day of my calamity; but the Lord was my stay and support.
>
> He brought me forth also into a large place; He was delivering me because He was pleased with me and delighted in me.
>
> The Lord rewarded me according to my righteousness (my conscious integrity and sincerity with Him); according to the cleanness of my hands has He recompensed me.

God uses troubles and struggles to enlarge us as people to prepare us for the "larger" position that He has for us. *God is always preparing us for what He has prepared for us!*

A time of great increase lies ahead for every believer who follows the Lord's leading and keeps the Lord's directives—and does so with great sensitivity and obedience to the Lord's timing.

We must be prepared *internally* for the blessings that God has for us *externally*. We must have the increased knowledge, understanding, wisdom, maturity, and experience necessary for handling increased responsibility, increased privilege, increased wealth, increased fame, or increased power.

Our talents and skills must become enlarged so we can make good decisions with our enlarged "place" in life.

There's yet one more enlargement that occurs. Psalm 18:36 tells us, "You enlarged my path under me; So that my feet did not slip." (NKJV)

The Lord brings us to an enlarged place so He might use us even more. He enlarges the path—the purpose, the ministry, the influence for good—that He has for us. We are not brought to a large place in order to become a bad example and a bad influence on others. No! We are brought to an enlarged position to influence, benefit, and bless others.

Through the years, and through many experiences of distress and difficulty, and through an increasing series of "enlargements," David finally was brought to the place where he was named King of Judea. After a period of kingship in Hebron, he became king over all Israel and moved his capital to Jerusalem. After a period of kingship there, he extended Israel's borders so that he was king over even greater territory. David's entire adult life is an example of these progressive stages of enlargement: enlarged difficulties result in enlarged saints who are led to enlarged places so they might walk an enlarged path with enlarged steps.

Enlarged Steps

The enlargement of our steps occurs as we make the right responses to life's experiences. Enlarged difficulties can lead to discouragement, which can lead to diminishment, which can lead to paralysis.

We must never fall into the error of believing that experience alone "enlarges" our capacity. An experience is only beneficial if you make the right response to experience! Your response to a circumstance in your life is what makes any experience a good one or bad one, a beneficial "growing" experience or a debilitating "withering" experience.

Let me give you an example. A flood rises and wipes out your home. That's an experience in your life. How do you respond to it? You can sit down and cry and say, "All is lost!" and live in a state of bitterness and disappointment the rest of your days. Or you can rise up and say, "I am still alive!" and pursue rebuilding your life in a positive way. How you respond will give full definition to that "experience" down the line.

What is the worst experience you have ever had? How did you respond to it? If you responded to it with faith and integrity, you are probably going to be able to say, "The worst experience I ever had actually turned out to be the greatest experience I ever had."

The people in Enterprise, Alabama came to believe just that. In 1915, the Mexican bollweevil invaded southeast Alabama with devastating results—sixty percent of the cotton crop was destroyed. The entire area experienced economic disaster.

As a result of that bollweevil invasion, however, the farmers diversified their farming and placed greater and greater emphasis on raising peanuts. This new crop brought great prosperity, and in two years the county in which Enterprise is located harvested more peanuts than any county in the nation. The citizens of Enterprise were so grateful for the bollweevil that they erected a monument to the insect—it has been described as the only monument ever dedicated to a pest. The monument bears the inscription, "In profound appreciation of the bollweevil and what it has done as the herald of prosperity."

A terrible time of trouble yielded a great enlargement!

Not too long ago I met a woman who had gone through a painful divorce. It was the worst experience of her life to be rejected by the man she loved and then discover things about him that made her realize that he wasn't at all the person she had thought he was. But...that experience drove her to study the Word of God as she had never studied it, to pray more than she had ever prayed, to open herself up to her Christian friends in new ways, and to discover new things about herself. She emerged from that experience a more vibrant and more accomplished woman with a much deeper, stronger, and richer relationship with the Lord. She praises God that He brought her through that experience. What the devil had meant for her demise turned out to be the opportunity for God's blessings.

We see this again and again in the Scriptures. Men and women of God find themselves in dire circumstances—they encounter terrible situations and suffer through nightmare-like "experiences." What they do in those times and how they handle those experiences, however, results in great testimonies to God's faithfulness.

Having "experience" is not enough. To say, "I've been down that road" is not a credential. The questions to ask of others and ourselves are these: What was learned from that experience? What was the net benefit or effect of that experience? How was God allowed to manifest Himself in that experience? What came out of that experience—was it positive or negative?

It is as you respond to life's circumstances and experiences in a positive, faith-filled, obedient manner that those experiences work to enlarge your steps...and to enlarge your wisdom.

Enlarged Wisdom

The positive enlargement of our steps refers to an increase in wisdom.

Many times I see new believers in Christ take large steps in their zeal and enthusiasm for what the Lord has done in their lives. Those steps are rarely maintained, however. What is birthed in a great deal of fervor and desire becomes tempered by practicalities, sometimes hindered by persecutions, and shaped by time and ongoing circumstances. Most people find that their initial soaring in Christ gives way to a rather routine pattern of "walking out" or "living out" the basic spiritual disciplines of reading the Word, praising the Lord, praying to the Lord, fellowship and worship with other believers, and service to those who are without Christ or who are in need. The Christian life can seem to become ordinary.

An amazing thing happens, however, to those who continue to "walk out" the basics of their relationship with the Lord day in, day out, week in, week out, month in, month out, year in, and year out. I'm not talking about an idle stroll or a neglectful, half-hearted walk. I'm talking about a diligent, concerted, focused, intentional, consistent walk. Those who continue to press forward in their walk with the Lord find that they become deeper in their understanding of the Scriptures. The Bible is far more than a book they read. The truths of the Bible become the very way they *think*, and out of their renewed thinking, the truths of the Bible become the impetus for their actions and behavior—what they do and say. Their relationship with the Lord becomes more precious and more vital. Their praise is more spontaneous. Their prayers are deeper, longer, and more effective. Their desire to reach out to others grows. They are quicker to witness about their relationship with Jesus Christ, bolder in encouraging or admonishing fellow believers, and more eager to pray with others or help shoulder the burdens of others. The character of Christ is forged within them—not in a moment, but in the course of the "walking."

And then there comes a day when the steps of that person are once again enlarged, this time with zeal that is tempered with the deep wisdom of God. What they do and say is more effective than anything they have done or said in times past. What they undertake is more focused in purpose, more powerful in expression, and more rewarding in results. They do not take the steps of a young sprinter bursting with enthusiasm, rather the long smooth strides of an experienced marathon runner. Their steps are sure and steady and smooth-flowing.

They move with poise and grace, knowing without doubt that God is in control of their lives and that His plans and purposes are for their eternal good. They know if they fall, He will be there to help them rise again. They know if they stumble, He will help steady them. They know if they take a wrong turn, He will put them back on track. They know if they fail, He will be there to instruct and redirect them. They know that if they become weary, He will give them encouragement.

They are walking in the enlarged steps of wisdom.

Enlarged Vision

I especially like George Barna's definition of vision: Vision is insight based on hindsight and accompanied by foresight. It is having a clear mental image of a wonderful, preferred future given to us by God to accomplish His plan on this earth. To have a vision from God empowers us. It gives us a sense of divine authority that we are not only to pursue the goals God sets before us, but that we will succeed in attaining those goals if we are faithful to God's call.

Unfortunately, we prefer to see God's vision through the eyes of our own will. We want to help determine how the vision is to unfold. We want a part in planning the details.

"Vision is insight based on hindsight and accompanied by foresight."
—George Barna

Sacrifice strips away self and puts us into a position to see *God's plan* through *God's eyes.*

Those who go through a test, make necessary sacrifices, and come to the point of total-life obedience find that they experience an enlarged vision of God, themselves, their relationship with God, and the tasks to which God is calling them.

The purpose of every test and its subsequent sacrifice and obedience is to move us to a new and enlarged level of strength, endurance, reliability, trust, faith, and increase.

It is at this point that the fulfillment of the promise comes into sharper focus. We are much more sure of what it is that God desires for us to be and do. We have an eternal perspective of life—we no longer are tossed about by daily circumstances or overwhelmed by daily stresses. We see the "big picture" of what God is desiring to do in us, through us, for us, and all around us.

It is also at this point that our faith is heightened to the point where we can *see* ourselves receiving the fulfillment of God's promise. It is as real to us as if it has already come to pass. We know that we know. We are sure of our salvation, certain of our call, and absolute in our convictions. We have an abiding calm deep within because we are resolute in our trust in God and our belief that God is going to be true to His Word and bring us victoriously into the place and position He desires for us to occupy.

Chapter 15

Choosing Increase

The fulfillment of God's promise occurs in our lives at God's precise timing, according to God's specified methods, and always for the furtherance of His Kingdom on this earth—both in our lives and in the lives of all others who are involved in the task to which He has called us. The fulfillment of God's promises occurs to bring God greater glory and to mold us more into the likeness of Christ Jesus His Son. God does not bring us to fulfillment simply so we might "feel good" or "feel better about ourselves." God brings about the fulfillment of His promises so we might have an enlarged witness that will influence others to accept His Son as their Savior.

The fulfillment of God's promise in our lives enlarges us. It gives us a new degree of capacity, confidence in the Lord, spiritual authority, and greater influence. It enlarges our reputation for Christ. It enlarges our wisdom, our faith, and our vision.

The fulfillment of God's promise enlarges His own position of triumphant power on this earth. The establishment of a promise on this earth is part of God's ongoing creative process—a dazzling display of His ability to take what is not and produce what is.

What a marvelous thing to experience the fulfillment of God's increase in our lives!

And yet...not every person who has an opportunity to move into increase chooses to do so. That may seem strange to you, but it is true nonetheless. Countless people choose to remain in a position of decrease, pain, turmoil, or trouble. Their choice may be conscious or subconscious—it is a choice nonetheless.

When you move into the land—the position, the role, the destiny—that God has for you, you will redeem that position or role fully. It will not be a place of decrease, depression, or humiliation for you, rather it will be a place of increase and success.

By the power of His Word, the Lord can change any place of depression into a place of joy!

So many people pray, "Oh, God, deliver me from this place, this job, this situation, this marriage, this circumstance, this condition." Our prayer should be, "Oh, God, deliver me IN this place, job, situation, marriage, circumstance, or condition! Bring about Your deliverance in the innermost recesses of my being. Set me free on the inside, enlarge me in spirit, encourage me, build me up spiritually, emotionally, and mentally, and enrich me in the inner man. Bring about Your righteousness, Your holiness, Your peace, Your joy, and Your holiness in my life. Bring me to the place where I am victorious on the inside regardless of my outside circumstances."

Trust God to change you. As you are changed, it is entirely likely that you will see your outer circumstances in a completely new light, you will be given strength to endure those circumstances, or you will be shown ways in which to change your circumstances. One of those three things happens to every believer I have ever met who first became victorious, joyful, and filled with praise, hope, and faith on the inside. The believer has a change of perspective, a new surge of power, and new insights about how to change outer conditions.

The fact is that good is always the worst enemy of best.

Genuine and lasting changes rarely begin with an outer change of condition, rather an inner change of heart! Such an inner change is possible only if you want this change in your life. It comes as you ask God for it. It does not come to you automatically or apart from your will.

Oh, how many people are in that position today! They like the idea of increase, they want to associate with successful people, or they want what they know rather than risk entering into what they do not know. They are willing to compromise God's best for something that is "good."

The fact is that good is always the worst enemy of best. Settling for good is what keeps most people from experiencing what is best in their lives.

Many people today, including many people in the church, have settled for what is good. They don't truly want the fullness of all God has for them.

Why Do We Say "No" to Increase?

Consider for a moment what God had promised to His people. He had told them that they would live in houses they had not built and take over fields they had not plowed. God had said they would take over storehouses that were full. Furthermore, God had promised to multiply the wealth of the land as they occupied it.

Caleb and Joshua were the only two of the twelve spies sent into Canaan who lived to cross over and possess Canaan. They were the only two who believed what God had said to them and believed that God was able to help them prevail over the inhabitants of the land promised to the Israelites. Caleb and Joshua were the only two who were willing to yield their entire lives, including all of their future, into the hands of God. They were willing to give God complete control.

Most of us do not like to give God control of our lives—or we think we have given Him control when, in actuality, we have only given Him control over Sundays. Many people seem to live in a state of nearly constant bargaining with God in which they attempt to give God the minimal amount of control over their lives to supposedly "keep God happy." The fact is that God desires all of your life—there is no room to compromise.

God has such a wonderful plan designed for your life—He has incredible designs for working in you, through you, and for you. What God does in us, He wants to reflect through us! We are the ones who are reluctant to receive and live out God's plan when, in truth, His plan is the only plan that will bring us the maximum amount of joy, peace, fulfillment, satisfaction, and increase!

Most people believe that if they work hard, work smart, and strive for success, they will eventually achieve their day in the sun. Actually, most people only seem to believe they may achieve success since they aren't really sure if success is possible for every person who "plays by the rules."

God says in sharp contrast, "Love Me, serve Me, do what it is that I designed for you and have planned for you, and you will have all that you ever desire without striving."

God's plan does not preclude hard work. Work is a part of our human lives. It does not eliminate "thinking smart." God designed us with brains and He intends for us to use them. Striving, however, is not a part of God's plan. He does not intend for us to live over-stressed, over-booked, worried, anxious, driven-for-success lives.

When we strive to do things our way and in our timing, oh, what a precarious position we are in! It is an ominous day and a day to be avoided in which God says to you, "I'm going to let you do it your way; I'm going to let you have your choice." Your way can never equal God's way, much less be better than God's way. God, however, will allow you to settle for second best, third best, or hundredth best, if that is your will. He has given you free will with which to choose your way or His. He will allow you to go your own way. It will always be a way, however, without the full blessing of God's increase.

A Forward Move Requires Faith

Stop to think about how finite man's understanding will always be. What does man really know when it comes to what God says? Very little.

We see things from a highly limited perspective. We have finite knowledge, finite viewpoints, and finite wisdom. We are locked into finite time. We live in a finite world, often hemmed in by man-made boundaries, protocols, definitions, and procedures.

To move from what we know in the finite realm to what God sees in the infinite realm takes faith. To move from what we know into the place God calls us to dwell requires taking the risk that God will be true to His Word, that God is total goodness, and that God loves without measure.

When you refuse to move forward in your faith to enter into the full increase God has for you, you bring discouragement to others around you. Even if you don't say a word, your example influences them to "settle" for something less than God's best. A choice to stay in the known realm of good, rather than move into the unknown realm that God calls "best," is not a private choice— it is a choice that impacts every person around you. And if you are a believer in Christ Jesus, your choice impacts the Kingdom of God in ways you probably haven't recognized or acknowledged.

Some time ago my son told me about a friend of his who had married at a very young age. The marriage turned out to be a troubled one. My son didn't seem surprised at the troubles in the marriage. In fact, he told me that he had predicted these troubles and had counseled his friend against the marriage. I asked my son why his friend had gone ahead and married the girl. His two-word reply said it all: "He settled."

To settle for something that you define and you choose without consulting the Lord or without accepting the challenge of the Lord to wait for, fight for, or pursue His best is always to settle for something that will have more problems associated with it than you ever imagined. That certainly turned out to be the case for Gad, Reuben, and Manasseh in the years that followed.

The descendants of these tribes experienced great difficulties for staying on the east side of the Jordan. They were greatly diminished by warring invaders and were brought into submission before foreign kings.

To make a choice *not* to enter into increase may actually be a choice to enter into decrease.

Chapter 16

Increase Out of Decrease

Some time ago I was in prayer about my family and our ministry together. My wife and I were grappling with a situation we considered to be a very big "negative" in our lives. Our daughter, who lived with us and was an integral part of our ministry, married and moved to New Zealand—just about the farthest place on the earth she could have moved! Our son, who lives in Tennessee and has traveled rather extensively in his own music ministry for a number of years, became engaged to a girl from Australia. My wife Shirley and I remained in Toledo, Ohio.

I said to the Lord, "I did not raise up my children in order to live apart from them forever. I did not raise my children to never see them when they became adults. I don't mind releasing them to their spouses and to their destinies, but I do not intend to live without them in my life."

The Lord dropped this thought into my heart as I prayed:

*That which you accept you will
no longer be challenged to change.*

I thought about that phrase in the light of a number of people I have known through the years who were diagnosed with cancer. It seems that at the outset, most of these people, when asked about their health, referred to "the cancer." It was an alien entity to them—an invader, a foe. They were determined to conquer the disease.

Over time, however, many of these people began to refer to the cancer as "my cancer." They had personalized the disease and had accepted it—indeed, they seemed to have possessed it. They were no longer as determined to reject or conquer the disease as much as they were resolved to "accept" whatever might happen to them.

In so many instances, we experience setbacks and negative forces coming against us, and our immediate response to them is, "I must fight this!" We are determined to push away what we know to be the enemy of our lives. We immediately discern that the enemy of our souls has moved against us in some way to steal from us, destroy us, or kill us. (See John 10:10.)

But then the attack becomes a "condition." When we are unable to reverse the negative financial situation, a condition of lack, loss, or poverty sets in—not only in the reality of our material possessions, but in our minds and hearts. We begin to think of ourselves as wanting or without.

When we are unable to beat the disease or conquer the obstacles to our health in the aftermath of an injury, we begin to think of ourselves as sick.

When we are unable to resolve differences in a relationship or to overcome deep-seated anger, bitterness, or resentment, we begin to regard our relationship as broken or estranged. We begin to think of ourselves as "separated" from the person.

We begin to own the thing that has struck our lives to our detriment. Once you accept something, you feel no reason to change it, rather you opt to "just live with it."

If you accept the fact that you have lost an opportunity or lost a dream, it is highly likely that you will never be open to pursuing a similar opportunity in the future or dream a similar dream again.

That which you accept you will
no longer be challenged to change.

I do not believe that God ever intended for us to accept a negative situation and call it our own. We should continue to refer to *the* cancer, *the* bankruptcy, *the* loss, *the* problem, *the* conflict, or *the* turmoil without any "my" or "our" possessive language.

"But," you may say, "isn't that living in denial?"

No. It's living in faith. Certainly bad things happen to us—yes, bad things happen even to good people. We should recognize them as bad and call them bad. But we should never allow those things to create our identity, define us, or invade our minds, hearts, and souls to the point that we *accept* the bad as being permanently associated with us.

For the believer in Christ Jesus, even the very worst of any situation in life is *only for a season.* Life is a wisp of time. No matter how bad things may be or may become, very soon all bad things will come to an end for the believer. To own a problem or disease is to say, "This is part of me and I will no longer seek to defeat it, get rid of it, be healed of it, or overcome it."

What we accept, we no longer feel challenged to fight or to change.

I have even met people who have so internalized and accepted negative situations in their lives that they don't know how to let loose of those situations, even after the negative outward conditions have passed. Some people continue to regard themselves as sick long after they have been cured of a particular disease or overcome a particular sickness. Some continue to see themselves as poor long after their debts are paid and they have positive cash flow in their lives. Others continue to see themselves as unworthy or without value long after they have acquired new friends or a spouse who truly loves them.

We must learn to let loose from what the Lord seeks to deliver us!

That which you accept, you will no longer be challenged to change.

The Lord also said to my heart, "As long as you are challenged by this absence from your children, you will do something about it." And we have. We met with our children and made a commitment as a family that we would find ways to bridge the miles. We renewed our commitment to express our feelings and ideas openly with one another. We made a commitment to frequent communication by means of telephone and internet messages. We made plans for travel—on some occasions for them to travel to the United States, on other occasions for us to travel to New Zealand. We refused to accept absence from one another as a permanent condition in our lives.

A Daily Courageous Walk in Faith

One of the foremost people in the Bible who walked faithfully day by day was Joshua. For some forty years, Joshua served as the right hand of Moses. He was second in command and, to a great extent, lived in the shadow of Moses. He lived to serve that great man of God.

But then the day came after Moses' death when the Lord said to Joshua that because he had been faithful, He was going to bless him and prosper him and he was going to be successful beyond his wildest imagination. He promised Joshua that every place he put his foot, he would claim that territory for God's people. He told him that no person would be his equal in authority or power as long as he lived. He gave Joshua the full assurance that He would be with him always—that He would neither fail nor forsake him.

What did God require of Joshua?

Courage and faithfulness.

The wellspring of Joshua's courage and faithfulness was to be the law. The Lord said,

> Be strong and very courageous, that you may
> do according to all the law which Moses My
> servant commanded you. Turn not from it to the
> right hand or to the left, that you may prosper
> wherever you go.

> This Book of the Law shall not depart out of
> your mouth, but you shall meditate on it day and
> night, that you may observe and do according to
> all that is written in it. For then you shall make
> your way prosperous, and then you shall deal
> wisely and have good success. (Josh. 1:7–8)

What does the Lord require of you?

The very same thing He required of Joshua! He commands you to be courageous and to be faithful to His Word. He requires that you draw your confidence not from your own strength and ability, but from His strength and His ability. He requires that you draw your wisdom not from yourself, but from His Word. He requires that you build your life upon His commandments. To do that, you must *know* His commandments with your mind, *believe* His commandments in your heart, and *keep* His commandments in your day-to-day living. You must DO what the Lord tells you to do.

To be courageous does not mean to simply muster up courage for an occasional bold or brave act. It means to be constant, steadfast, and never wavering. It means to live out God's commandments regardless of what others may think, say, or do. It means to boldly live out God's life on this earth in spite of rejection, ridicule, or a lack of response from certain people. To be courageous means to be loyal to the Lord...to submit to the Lord in all areas of your life...and to take on the enemy of your soul in spiritual warfare day by day.

Most people have good definitions for the words constancy, loyalty, and submission. But few of us really ARE constant, loyal, and submissive to God at all times. To be constant, loyal, and submissive takes inner fortitude and steadfastness—it takes *courage.*

The writer to the Hebrews echoed this same message:

> Be ever mindful of the days gone by in which,
> after you were first spiritually enlightened, you
> endured a great and painful struggle,

Sometimes being yourselves a gazingstock,
publicly exposed to insults and abuse and distress,
and sometimes claiming fellowship and making
common cause with others who were so treated.

For you did sympathize and suffer along with
those who were imprisoned, and you bore
cheerfully the plundering of your belongings and
the confiscation of your property, in the knowledge
and consciousness that you yourselves had a better
and lasting possession.

Do not, therefore, fling away your fearless
confidence, for it carries a great and glorious
compensation of reward.

For you have need of steadfast patience and
endurance, so that you may perform and fully
accomplish the will of God, and thus receive and
carry away [and enjoy to the full] what is promised.
(Heb. 10:32–36)

Each of us has a need of steadfast patience and endurance!

Perseverance to Outlast Persecution. Perseverance will
always outlast persecution. One person with commitment,
persistence, and endurance can accomplish more than a thousand
people who are only "wishful" in their dreaming. To be an
achiever, you must always reach for that which is just beyond
your grasp. That's the realm of faith. Faith is the bridge between
today's reality and tomorrow's vision.

Abraham was called by God to walk out the land of Canaan
as his inheritance. While Abraham was living in Haran, the Lord
said to him:

Go for yourself [for your own advantage] away
from your country, from your relatives and your
father's house, to the land that I will show you.

And I will make of you a great nation, and I
will bless you [with abundant increase of favors]

and make your name famous and distinguished, and you shall be a blessing [dispensing good to others].

And I will bless those who bless you [who confer prosperity or happiness upon you] and curse him who curses or uses insolent language toward you; in you will all the families and kindred of the earth be blessed [and by you they will bless themselves]. (Gen. 12:1–3)

The Lord also said very specifically to Abraham: "I will give this land to your posterity." (Gen. 12:7)

Did Abraham live to see all this happen? No. He died a wanderer in the land. He did not see his son Isaac possess the land fully. He did not see his seed become a "great nation." He did not see the full extent of the way in which he was a blessing to others or that they were blessed by blessing him.

> *One person with commitment, persistence, and endurance can accomplish more than a thousand people who are only "wishful" in their dreaming.*

Did that keep Abraham from walking in faith and serving the Lord God as he walked out the land? Far from it. Abraham believed in the promise. It gave him hope for his future and the future of those who would come after him. He believed in the *reality* of the promise...he walked as if he was already living in the certainty of its fulfillment. And as he walked out the land and lived out his years, he *was* blessed. He saw the miracle birth of his son Isaac to his barren wife Sarah. He saw the provision of God repeatedly through the years. He heard the voice of God and had a true "friendship" with God. We read in Genesis 24:1, "The Lord had blessed Abraham in all things."

A great blessing comes to those who continue to hold out hope for the fulfillment of God's promises, even though they may not receive them in the timing or in the ways they had anticipated.

It is a blessing that comes in the form of things eternal, not temporal. It is a blessing that cannot be quenched and cannot be stolen. It is a blessing that is as sure as the reality on which it is based.

Abraham never returned to Haran, nor did he return to Ur. He never gave up on God's call to him. He never wavered in his pursuit of God's promise.

One of the greatest testaments to any person's faith is the fact that they do not return to sin, even in times of temptation or discouragement. To me, that is an even more powerful testimony than the testimony of the person who fully receives a promise from God.

Every generation of believers exists, to a certain degree, in a suspended state of delayed gratification. We continue to build, work, believe, and witness with the *hope* of the *fulfillment* of the promise of the Lord's return to this earth.

Because we have not yet experienced the Lord's return, does that mean that we should not hold on to the hope that has been handed down to us through the generations? Absolutely not. We must not only cherish and cling to that hope, but we must instill that hope in our children and grandchildren. Why? Because the *promise* of Christ's return is a sure and certain promise in God's Word. It *will* be realized on this earth in the fullness of God's timing. Our part *may* be to receive the fullness of that promise...but if the Lord continues to delay His coming in His mercy and forbearance with mankind, we also may *not* receive the fullness of that promise. Is that cause for abandoning the promise? No! The promise is a reality from God's perspective— it is an absolute certainty. The promises of God are to be embraced and believed fully. They are the firm foundation on which our hope is built.

The same is true for all other promises of God's Word. The genuine promises of God in the Scriptures are rock solid and eternal. They do not change. We may experience the fullness of a promise in the near future...in the distant future...or in the eternal future. We do not know precisely when the promise will be fully experienced by us. Nevertheless, we can know with our faith that the promise *will* become a reality in our lives, even if that fulfillment comes in eternity.

Choose to walk courageously today.
Choose to walk faithfully.
Increase *will* come.

Chapter 17

Responding to Increase

God will not share His glory with man.

Furthermore, He is worthy to be praised at all times regardless of how *we* think God should act. We always must remain keenly aware that when we experience increase, the normal human tendency is to say, "I brought this about." We like to point to specific things we said, actions we took, plans we made, and arguments we won. We like to take credit for the good investments we have made, the wise moves we took, and our astute responses to passing opportunities.

Pride can easily set in.

When pride sets in, two things we result. First, we tend to forget God's commandments. Second, we stop giving God our thanks and praise.

I am continually amazed at those who rise in power or fame who suddenly conclude that certain aspects of God's law no longer pertain to them. They think that because they are elected to certain offices or function in a certain level of God's anointing that they can overlook certain aspects of God's law and get away with disobedience. They seem to believe that certain commandments no longer apply to them—they see themselves as being "above" God's law.

Let me assure you that no person is ever above God's commandments.

Others believe they are beyond any need to give God offerings of thanksgiving and praise. They draw the assumption that they have become wealthy solely on their own wit and wisdom. They, therefore, no longer believe they owe God thanks or praise for what they possess. Moses knew this tendency existed and he said,

> Beware lest you say in your [mind and] heart, My power and the might of my hand have gotten me this wealth.
>
> But you shall [earnestly] remember the Lord your God, for it is He Who gives you power to get wealth, that He may establish His covenant which He swore to your fathers, as it is this day. (Deut. 8:17–18)

Closely related to this tendency to forget God's commandments and to stop thanking and praising Him is a tendency to turn away from the truth of His covenant with man and to seek alternative forms of religion.

We find sobering words of caution in Deuteronomy 8:10–14 that deal with this very issue:

> When you have eaten and are full, then you shall bless the Lord your God for all the good land which He has given you.
>
> Beware that you do not forget the Lord your God by not keeping His commandments, His precepts, and His statutes which I command you today,
>
> Lest when you have eaten and are full, and have built goodly houses and live in them,
>
> And when your herds and flocks multiply and your silver and gold is multiplied and all you have is multiplied,

> Then your [minds and] hearts be lifted up and
> you forget the Lord your God, Who brought you
> out of the land of Egypt, out of the house of
> bondage.

I have seen a significant number of people in my life who became successful and then decided that Christianity was too demanding of them. They didn't want to tithe or give offerings to God's work, they didn't want to keep all of the commandments of God, they didn't want to be "restricted" in any aspects of their behavior, and they didn't want to be locked in to going to church on certain days. At first the draw away from Christ was very subtle, but over time these people opted for an "easier" religion— the way established by Jesus Christ was too demanding on their own desire to control their own destiny and take credit for their own success.

Moses also knew that this tendency to move away from God to less demanding religions would exist once the Israelites experienced increase. He warned,

> If you forget the Lord your God and walk after
> other gods and serve them and worship them, I
> testify against you this day that you shall surely
> perish.
> Like the nations which the Lord makes to
> perish before you, so shall you perish, because
> you would not obey the voice of the Lord your
> God. (Deut. 8:19–20)

Our first response to God's increase must always be humble thanks and praise offered to God, our Source. We must continue to worship God and to obey Him.

Be a Blessing to Others

Our second response to God's increase must be our use of that increase to bless others.

There are no selfish blessings in the Kingdom.

God does not bless you so you can lavish possessions upon yourself. He does not place at your disposal resources for you to squander them upon your own pleasures. No! God blesses His people so they might be a blessing.

Remember what God said to Abram: "I will bless you [with abundant increase of favors] and make your name famous and distinguished, and you will be a blessing [dispensing good to others]." (Gen. 12:2)

The people to whom you are *first* to be a blessing are those who are in fellowship with you in Christ Jesus. In Ephesians 4:16 we read,

> For because of Him the whole body (the church, in all its various parts), closely joined and firmly knit together by the joints and ligaments with which it is supplied, when each part [with power adapted to its need] is working properly [in all its functions], grows to full maturity, building itself up in love.

You must recognize that you have been "fitted into" the Body of Christ. You are a joint or ligament—you link together other members of the Body even as they are joined to you. The purpose for your place in the Body of Christ is to do divine *work*.

God does not place you in the Body of Christ solely so you will feel good about yourself or feel secure in His love, although both of those results occur. God has something for you to *do*.

As you love those to whom you are joined—which in a practical way means to *give* of your substance, talents, gifts, and time to those to whom you are linked—two things happen simultaneously. First, needs are met. And second, the Body as a whole grows into full spiritual maturity in Christ.

When you give of your substance and your giftings to others, you are used by God to meet a need in their lives. You, in turn, are built up as you receive from the substance and the giftings they give to you. The greater this flow of giving and receiving out of love, the greater the Body grows spiritually. There is a mutual giving and receiving of individual contributions that builds up the whole and meets the needs of the whole, as well as the needs of individual members.

Increase does not occur in isolation. It is intended to be a whole-Body-of-Christ experience.

The only people God has to work through on this earth are those who believe in Him and in His Son, Jesus Christ. They are the ones who are active, live vessels of God's power.

Next time you go to church, look around and say to yourself, "These are the people with whom God intends for me to have a giving and receiving relationship. These are the people I am to bless. These are the people from whom I am to receive blessing."

The Holy Spirit desires that every gift that God has given *to* you has an opportunity to flow *through* you to others. His gifts are not intended to be hoarded by you, but to be used by you for the benefit of others. Certainly your needs are met and you are blessed and increased in the process, but no gift given to you by the Holy Spirit—material or spiritual—is intended for you to keep solely for your own use.

I firmly believe there is a direct correlation between what you and I give into the Body of Christ, and very specifically into the church of which we are a part, and the amount of the anointing of the power of Jesus Christ that is released into that Body. Those churches that have the greatest amount of giving and receiving in their membership—with an overflowing generosity and joy accompanying freely shared gifts, talents, and resources—are the churches that experience the greatest number of souls saved, the greatest number of miracles, and the greatest growth. The supply of the power and presence of Jesus Christ is in direct proportion to the supply of the "gifts" that are given from the membership.

Again, these gifts are not merely financial, although they include finances. Gifts include the totality of spiritual and natural talents, gifts, resources, and contributions of time and service.

This does not mean that there is an increase in the anointing—the anointing of God is unlimited, infinite, and all-powerful. It means that there is an increase in the release of that anointing in a particular Body.

God is not passive. He is aggressive—and not only that, He is progressive. God is always moving toward us, seeking ways in which He can give to us, help us, and bless us. We are the ones who back away from God. We are the ones who reject His mercy and forgiveness. We are the ones who are hesitant to follow Him quickly and decisively. We are the ones who are reluctant to move out into the areas in which He desires to lead us.

Outreach to Those Lost and in Need

A noted economist recently stated in a national publication that there has never been a time of economic growth such as we have known in the last eighteen years—not only in the United States, but in foreign nations as well. Furthermore, there is no explanation as to why the overall world economy has manifested such unprecedented energy and growth.

An acquaintance of mine in the construction industry echoed this opinion as he told me his plans for a ten-day vacation: "I have never experienced in all my years of building what I have experienced in the last seven years. I haven't taken a day of vacation for seven years. There has simply been more to build than adequate time to build and skilled workmen to do the jobs. Finally, I decided that there wasn't going to be a 'good time' to take a vacation so I simply walked away from the office and said, 'Don't try to reach me for any reason other than a death.'"

Economists estimate that more people will become millionaires in the first decade of the twenty-first century than in any ten-year period in the history of the world. Money is flowing, business is flourishing, and economies are expanding.

I believe that for any manifestation in the natural world, we can find a preceding manifestation in the spiritual realm. Very specifically, an increase in material prosperity only occurs after

---

God is always moving toward us,
seeking ways in which He can give to
us help us, and bless us.

---

an increase of spiritual power and intensity. It is only after God decides and declares that something will manifest on the earth that it manifests.

In Isaiah 9, the Lord speaks through the prophet Isaiah to foretell the day when the people who have walked in darkness will see a great light, the yoke of Israel's burden will be broken, and a child will be born whose name will be called Wonderful Counselor, Mighty God, Everlasting Father, Prince of Peace. And then we read these powerful words:

> Of the increase of His government and of peace
> there shall be no end, upon the throne of David
> and over his kingdom, to establish it and to uphold
> it with justice and with righteousness from the
> [latter] time forth, even for evermore. The zeal of
> the Lord of hosts will perform this. (Isa. 9:7)

Government in this passage does not refer merely to political or legal forces. It refers to all authority, including authority over economic forces, health-related factors, knowledge factors, and spiritual forces.

For those of us who believe in Jesus Christ, the "government" of our life is the Lord Himself. He is our Master and we are His servants. He lives within us and He is producing increase in us. There is no end to the increase God desires for you. He desires for you an ever-growing increase of love, peace, joy, and fulfillment.

This increase wells up within you first and then overflows into your external life.

What is the driving force behind this increase? Isaiah 9:7 gives us the clear answer. The *Lord of hosts* will perform it! The increase does not come about because of what a human being does. It occurs because of what God sets Himself to do.

Regardless of what any one person or group of people may do, God ultimately controls the purse strings of the world's finances. God can shut down an economy in a day. He can open the windows of heaven and pour out an overflowing blessing in a day. Behind any manifestation of increase you will always find "the zeal of the Lord of hosts."

Why are we experiencing a great increase around the world today? *Why* is there such an explosion of knowledge, businesses, and wealth?

Along with the increase of wealth in the world, there is an increase in the amount of money that is flowing into churches and ministries. Percentages in some areas may be down, but the overall dollar figure associated with churches and ministries around the world is greater than ever before. Why is there an unprecedented flow of money into the Kingdom of God?

In addition to this material increase, in the last one hundred years we have seen God restore to the church the gifts of healing, the gifts of the Holy Spirit, the full functioning of the offices of evangelist, prophet, and teacher in the church, and a great wave of praise and worship. *Why?*

Why is the most potent question we can ask about any major increase or decrease we experience, either individually or as the Body of Christ. What is God attempting to teach us or call us to do? What is God desiring to accomplish in us and through us and for us?

The clear fact of God's Word is that we are to be continually claiming new territory in the spirit realm with every passing year we live. We are to be building the Kingdom—extending the light of the Gospel into areas of darkness, establishing the righteousness of God in areas of evil and sin, and enlarging the influence and effectiveness of the church around the world.

It takes just as much faith to know how to handle a harvest as to believe God will send one. Ask God today to reveal to you the part He desires for you to have in the extension of His Kingdom.

There's nothing more wonderful than to see an increase of souls. That truly is the most fulfilling and satisfying harvest any person can experience.

Conclusion

Still More....

Do you like where you are today? Do you like the level of prosperity that you are experiencing in your spirit, soul, body, mind, relationships, and finances? Do you like who you are? What would you attempt if you knew you would not fail?

You will never become something other than what you are right now unless you know *what* you desire to be. You will never change your location until you determine your destination.

We each are motivated to become what we imagine ourselves to be.

The creating of an image is one of the most powerful things you can do. One of the wonderful things about the way our Creator made us is that we have the ability to create an image in our spirit and allow that image to drive us until we see its fulfillment. A person always moves in the direction of his most dominant thought. When you change an image and you make that new image your dominant thought, you will change your attitude and behavior to line up with the new image. Changes in attitude and behavior then fuel changes in feelings. You will inevitably express what you consistently envision and expect.

What would you attempt if you knew you would not fail?

The goal that lies ahead for every Christian is to create an image that lines up with the *whole* of God's Word, the Bible. Don't allow anyone other than God to create an image of failure—or success—for you. That image will be false in some way because it is prone to human error and finite judgment. Only the image that God has for you is true and eternal.

God's vision for your life is truly remarkable. No one else in the world is just like you. God programmed you to be genetically distinct from all other human beings. Your fingerprints, blood chemistry, and DNA all say you are one of a kind. God not only made you as a unique creation, but He set you in a unique time and environment. He has for you a very specific purpose for being—a step-by-step plan for becoming more and more like Christ Jesus and, thereby, impacting your present world in ways that are more and more miraculous.

If you don't know today just how unique you are...ask the Lord to reveal your individuality to you.

If you don't know today where God desires for you to live, work, and minister...look around. Ask the Lord to let you see your world the way He sees it. There are needs in every direction, and the place for you to start living, working, and ministering in your full potential is in the place where God has presently planted you.

If you don't know today your specific purpose for being—the uniqueness of your calling and the individual plan God has for you to fulfill—ask the Lord to reveal His plan to you. He may not reveal the entirety of it to you in one sudden burst of revelation. The truth is, such a revelation would scare most people. God will, however, reveal to you the character He desires for you to exemplify in this world. That *character* is found in fullness in Christ Jesus and is revealed fully to you in God's Word.

The specific things you are to do begin with the things God desires for you to do "next." Ask God for His plan for your today...for your tomorrow...for this week...for the immediate future. It is as you trust the Holy Spirit to guide you day by day that the Lord will lead you into your future. Do what the Holy Spirit convicts, compels, or challenges you to do *today*. Your obedience sets you on the right course for doing what the Holy Spirit convicts, compels, and challenges you to do *tomorrow*. Let each day unfold as the Spirit wills.

As the Holy Spirit reveals to you specific things He desires for you to say and do, be quick to respond. Seize the vision He lays out for you. Wrap your arms of faith around it and hold on to that vision. Do not waiver in your faith as you walk out what He has asked you to do.

Ask God to give you the courage you need to endure until the day your increase arrives. Make Psalm 37:3-5 your theme:

> Trust (lean on, rely on, and be confident) in the Lord and do good; so shall you dwell in the land and feed surely on His faithfulness, and truly you shall be fed.
>
> Delight yourself also in the Lord, and He will give you the desires and secret petitions of your heart.
>
> Commit your way to the Lord [roll and repose each care of your load on Him]; trust (lean on, rely on, and be confident) also in Him and He will bring it to pass.

Yes, He WILL bring it to pass!

Have you ever walked along a sidewalk in an older neighborhood and come across a portion of the slab that has been pushed up by the roots of a nearby tree? When you look at a root by itself, the root may appear flexible, even limp. It hardly *appears* to be able to move concrete. But when the force of the life of the tree is surging through that root, it is a powerful force.

So, too, are our lives when we are empowered by the Holy Spirit. The force of life within us—not our life, but His life at work in us—moves obstacles and oppositions and oppressions.

Job 23:10–14 gives us these encouraging words:

> He knows the way that I take;
> *When* He has tested me,
> I shall come forth as gold.
> My foot has held fast to His steps;
> I have kept His way and not turned aside.
> I have not departed from the commandment
> of His lips;
> I have treasured the words of His mouth
> More than my necessary *food*.
> But He is unique, and who can make Him change?
> And *whatever* His soul desires, *that* He does.
> For He performs *what is* appointed for me... (NKJV)

Yes, He WILL perform what is appointed for you!

Look for it to happen!

www.ingramcontent.com/pod-product-compliance
Lightning Source LLC
Chambersburg PA
CBHW051829090426
42736CB00011B/1718